洞月亮

CAVE MOON PRESS

YAKIMA 中 WASHINGTON

2019

So, Dear Writer ...

An It's About Time Writers' Reading
Series Anthology

洞月亮
CAVE MOON PRESS
YAKIMA 中 WASHINGTON

ISBN: 978-0-9797785-5-1

So, Dear Writer ...

An It's About Time Writers' Reading
Series Anthology

Table of Contents

Introduction

The *It's About Time Writer's Reading Series* Anthology brings together seventeen essays on the writer's craft that originated as talks at Seattle's *It's About Time Writers' Reading Series*. The monthly reading series, founded by writer and poet Esther Altshul Helfgott in January 1990, is our community's longest running series open to all readers and is dedicated to the memory of Anna Helfgott, (1899-1996) who began writing at age 70, & to the memory of Nelson Bentley (1918-1990), the quintessential teacher who gave Anna, & scores of others, help & hope. It's About Time is dedicated to an end of racism, homophobia, antisemitism, homelessness & war.

The vibrant and well-attended readings, now held at the Ballard Branch of The Seattle Public Library, each include featured readers, an open mic, and a talk by a seasoned writer on the writer's craft. Helfgott introduced the craft talks in January 2001. We have now enjoyed and learned from more than 220 craft talks. I am proud to note that I gave the first one, though at this writing, nineteen years later, I am unable to bring its subject matter to mind! But Esther took notes while listening to the talks, so you may find them in the University of Washington's Archives on the bottom level of Suzzallo library where she continues to deposit material in the It's About Time Writers' file.

What do we mean by craft? Here, in this manual, you have not rules but considerations, strategies, approaches, guidelines, and suggestions for use in writing poetry or fiction or memoir or anything else for that matter.

First comes the act of generating writing, because without a piece of writing to work on, well, there's nothing to do. Matt Briggs asks us to consider whether we want to write a competent story, using known moves and forms, or rather, to trek out into the unknown.

Rebecca Loudon advises reading—everything from the classic poets to cookbooks. She advises to always carry a notebook, to feel free to write about everything and anything, and to write every day the way a violinist practices every day.

Linda Clifton bids us poets to tell it true, to claim for ourselves accuracy, which involves a process of discovery and which is a form of resistance to the hackneyed and falsifying language that saturates our culture. Revision, says Clifton, is working to see more clearly. Sheila Bender guides us past the hesitations, bumps, doubts, and blocks that we may encounter on our way to finished pieces and poems.

Peter Pereira reflects on finding a subject. His practices include making time for contemplation, writing on a regular schedule, and learning to recognize when a subject has found you (because, he elaborates, you don't find a subject, your subject finds you, often at a completely inappropriate moment!).

Pamela Moore Dionne suggests ways to get to know your characters and then to get out of their way as they tell you their stories. David Messengill shares his experience of writing fiction for a decade, quitting because it didn't pay, and then—seeing how writing fiction was for him a necessary pursuit—beginning again on a better basis. His guidelines for a better basis apply to us all.

Laura Gamache, having walked into the country of cancer, where she did not know the language, speaks of transliteration—using the sounds of a language you don't know to find a poem of your own. Susan Rich also discusses finding subject matters, moving between poems of witness and poems of bread and wine—daily sensual experience. Rich gives us writing prompts to get us going.

Kay Mullen speaks to us about her Vietnamese son's return to Viet Nam, where he had not been since babyhood, and how poetry is one way to keep what has happened from slipping into oblivion. She shows how she maps a poem, looking for its geography and its "physical, emotional, intellectual and linguistic aspects."

Bethany Reid has devised the strategy of writing "one bad poem" each and every day. Why bad? Because to attempt to write a good or great poem every day is to attempt the impossible, and a "bad" poem can always be made into a good poem. Writing a "bad" poem every day is practical even for one with a full-time teaching job and three daughters to raise.

And now turning to the revision process. Mike Hickey gives us a list of fourteen points of advice on everything from punctuation to image, ending with the advice to ignore all such advice while writing the first draft. Just write! John McFarland thinks deeply about openings, as should we.

What to do once you have written, once you have completed poems or stories or essays? Michael Dylan Welch shares his file-card system for tracking poems being composed, sent out, rejected, and ultimately accepted. Any productive writer could use Welch's example and some form of his system. And I offer (in a later craft talk, not the unremembered first one) a system for tracking your works—everything brought to the point of first draft—partly to avoid losing half of them under the bed and partly to begin to see each new poem or story the way many world-class creators see their works—as part of a body of work being created over a lifetime.

Sandi Sonnenfeld relates how nourishing to the creative work it is to begin again at the beginning after a publishing success. And finally Tamara Sellman, in discussing whether entering an MFA (Master of Fine Arts) program is a necessary course of action for a writer (it is not), outlines practices writers can do for themselves that are as good or better than entering an MFA program. Sellman's suggested practices would enhance the working life of any writer, whether or not he, she, or they have a degree lying around in a drawer.

So, dear writer, welcome to a compendium of voices seasoned, insightful, and wise. Sample and browse and take what you need to stimulate and deepen your own creative endeavors.

Priscilla Long
Seattle
May 2019

Poetry Revision Checklist

Mike Hickey

July 11, 2002

Poetry is the art of revision. Occasionally poems arrive into the world complete like a birth with no labor pains. But the vast majority of poems have to be crafted ten times, twenty times as many times and over the course of as many weeks or months as necessary. What seems complete today usually isn't. One of the keys to quality revision is to tap into the same energy and creativity that spawned the poem in the first place. Then, as poet Thomas Lux says, you render the poem using different aesthetic glasses or "lenses" such as your punctuation lenses, diction lenses, syntax lenses, etc. Below is a list that you may find helpful. Good luck!

1. PUT THE POEM AWAY FOR A DAY OR TWO BEFORE YOU REVISE. This will increase your objectivity and sense of poetic distance—very helpful for discovering what your poem is really about.

2. BE ECONOMICAL. Eliminate any "unnecessary" words. You'd be surprised how many pronouns (I, me, we, they, you, etc.) can be cut without losing clarity. Articles—a, an, the—are also prime candidates for editing. Ideally, you should ask yourself this question about each and every word in your poem: Can I cut this without sacrificing clarity or creativity?

3. VERBS: Are you getting the most for your money? Bland verbs can often be weighing a poem down. Instead of "says," would something like "screams," "whispers," "bellows," etc. be more expressive? Also, be aware of using the "ing" (continuous) form of verbs. They tend to be far less crisp and vivid than simple present tense. Simple present tense is an advisable technique for all poems when possible, as it lends more

immediacy and intimacy to the writing, which allows the reader to be more of an active participant. It makes the poem feel like it is unfolding before their eyes. ADJECTIVES: Don't overdo it. One adjective is fine: two is usually pushing it; three is almost always over the top. ADVERBS: Most "ly" adverbs are unnecessary if the verb is strong enough. There are notable exceptions to this rule, such as Emily Dickinson's "*Because I could not stop for Death, /He kindly stopped for me;*" However, if your writing is peppered with adverbs, the language would be tighter if energetic verbs did more of the work.

4. THE TITLE, FIRST LINE, AND LAST LINE are three powerful components of almost every poem. Are you getting the most bang for your buck in these three elements?

5. TRY NOT TO REPEAT WORDS unless it is done for artistic effect. Casual repetition of words indicates a limited vocabulary to the reader.

6. READ THE POEM ALOUD. It is astonishing how poems can change when you HEAR them as opposed to just READ them. I have never found a writer who disagrees with this advice.

7. DON'T FALL IN LOVE WITH YOUR WRITING TO THE DE-GREE that you're reluctant to cut a "good" line. If it doesn't belong in the poem, and you know it, cut it and save it for something else. Also, if the poem stumbles upon an idea that is more compelling than the original concept, don't be afraid to abandon your original destination.

8. "LEAVE 'EM WITH AN IMAGE." Poetry depends heavily on sensory language. Visual imagery tends to create a lasting impression, like a branding iron. (This directly relates to the first commandment of writing: Thou Shalt Show, Not Tell.) Another possibility is to be a bit didactic. By the end of a good poem, the reader is eating out of your hand. Without going overboard and dropping an anvil on the reader's head,

this is your opportunity to reveal the theme, the lesson learned, the moral to the story. Still, it's best to be subtle.

9. OVERCOMING OBJECTIONS: Every poem is similar to selling a used car—readers are naturally skeptical. If something doesn't ring true to you, it probably won't to the reader either, which includes poetic clichés like the word "soul." This word was used extensively in Shakespeare's era and for hundreds of years after, so if you use it, proceed at your own risk!

10. LET SOMEONE ELSE READ YOUR WORK. No matter how meticulous you are, no one can pick out all the problems in their own writing. Find someone you trust artistically. Writing workshops are excellent because they provide a consensus as to what is successful and what is problematic. Friends and family members are often incapable of separating the poem from the poet and, therefore, usually make lousy critics. Find someone capable of determining what works as well as what does not. Also, it's a common phenomenon that the poem you think is great stuff isn't, and the poem you perceive as trash is really a treasure.

11. THERE ARE TWO TYPES OF GOOD WRITERS: Good writers & good re-writers. Try to determine what works best for you in the revision process—adding or cutting. Personally, I tend to throw in everything in the first draft and then edit. But many writers I know are the exact opposite. For them, the first draft is more of a blueprint or skeleton—and then they "flesh it out" later.

12. ATTEMPT TO DIFFERENTIATE BETWEEN poems and poetry "exercises." While some poetry exercises may not be effective as finished products (i.e. they aren't publishable), they are critical to your artistic development. Writing a poem about your divorce or the death of a loved one is an important and cathartic process that will improve your writing in the long run. In other words, don't be afraid to write a bad poem.

As the late poet William Stafford once said, some days you just have to lower your standards!

13. PUNCTUATION: Too many commas, periods, semi-colons, colons etc. are like roadblocks. Some poems need academic punctuation for clarity's sake, but many don't. Punctuation at the end of lines is usually unnecessary because the line break itself accomplishes the effect of allowing the reader to stop and breathe. While some may disagree, when it comes to punctuation, my rule of thumb is: less is more.

14. LAST BUT NOT LEAST (in fact, most important of all), COMPLETELY IGNORE STEPS 1 THRU 13 during the first draft. Poetry writing is composed of two main parts: a) Writing (vision) & b) Rewriting (revision). Don't allow these guidelines to impede the flow of your imagination. Unleash your creative voice. Then, after a gestation period, think about ways to improve what you've written.

Mike Hickey has received creative writing degrees from the University of Arizona and the University of Washington and has taught creative writing classes at the Experimental College and South Seattle Community College since 1993. He has published poetry and creative non-fiction in magazines such as *The Atlanta Review*, *The Seattle Review*, and *The Seattle Weekly*. Hickey spends his spare time volunteering as a poet/therapist with juvenile inmates at King County Youth Detention, and his second novel, *Tell Me What You Want*, is scheduled to be released this summer by Cricket Cottage Press.

Competency vs. Incompetency

Matt Briggs

August 8, 2002

There can be two ways of looking at the process of writing. There is a sort of writing as competency way of approaching it. A writer says, maybe, I want to learn how to write the kind of short story published in *The New Yorker*. So the writer learns all the components of the kind of story published in *The New Yorker*. Once she has them safely mastered she considers she has finished learning and begins to produce her stories. I think of this kind of writer sitting back once she is writing her safe stories, saying, "and it was during those years that I learned how to write." The process of learning has been accomplished and put behind the student writer. The writer has a confidence that when she sits down to write she will produce a finished short story that conforms more or less to her ideal of what a story ought to be.

The other kind of writing, I guess, could be called writing as incompetency. A writer might start from scratch or she might already know how to write the kind of short story published in *The New Yorker*, but the writer feels there is something about slapping together a story that produces a predictable, disingenuous result. This writer begins to mistrust any story produced using predictable routines. She understands that each time she sits down to write no matter how many stories she has already written, she is starting fresh and therefore risks failure. It isn't the product writers are relying on to validate their enterprises but their fluency in the writing process. They never finish learning, and would never consider themselves anything other than a student writer.

Naturally, I tend to admire writers who keep pushing themselves beyond their comfort zones as writers; however, I'm sympathetic to the impulse to write the kind of stories a writer already knows how to write. As a writer I hope to juggle these two competing impulses; it is simple to write the first way because the writer has successful models to examine and past successes to back her up. The second method is difficult to accomplish because the writer is the only one who can discover stories that haven't been written yet, but sometimes a writer just isn't interested in discovering anything new and just wants to tell her reader a story.

Literary fiction writers must understand it is all right to feel like they don't know what the hell they're doing; it is the sensation of incompetence, or as Donald Bartheleme calls it "Not-Knowing" that leads to original work. I understand the term literary fiction to be antithetical to genre fiction. One of the blunders a writer can make, I think, is to develop the genre of themselves. It is exciting to see writers escape themselves as writers. Thus Raymond Carver's short story "Errand" feels like an explosion from his self-imposed limitations as a writer producing readily identifiable stories in the Raymond Carver genre of short fiction. Or Rebecca Brown's story, "A Good Man" at the end of "Annie Oakely's Girl" where the sudden realism and depth of literal prose in Brown's normally lush metaphorical prose feels like an entirely new, clear-eyed universe opening up. Where, most writers develop into story-generating machines pumping out stories using identical modes of telling what they need to tell, writers like Borges, Ken Kalfus, Rebecca Brown, Ben Marcus, Melissa Pritchard, Donald Barthelme, and so on seem to struggle with fundamental issues of how to write what they write.

Matt Briggs is the author of eight works of fiction including *The Remains of River Names* and *Shoot the Buffalo*. Dr. Cicero Books will release, *Frog in My Throat*, a collection of very short stores in 2017. Kevin Killian writes of the collection, "They borrow some of the pleasurable novelty factor the early Modernists enjoyed—Gertrude Stein, Jean Toomer,

Raymond Roussel, Ronald Firbank, Katherine Mansfield—a delight in the materials around us, even when they're as grim as the menus of Olive Garden." Briggs's writing has been awarded The American Book Award, *The Stranger* Genius Award, and The Nelson Bentley Prize in Fiction from *The Seattle Review*.

The Writer's Craft

Rebecca Loudon

February 13, 2003

My dictionary describes craft as: a strength, a special skill particularly in the arts, a skill in deceiving or underhanded planning, or a boat, ship or aircraft.

I think all of these descriptions are applicable when it comes to poetry. Certainly it takes strength and skill. It also takes a certain amount of deception, or, if you will, magic, to convince your reader to suspend disbelief, to put themselves aside in order to step into the strange little life of your poem. And most importantly, the idea of craft as a boat. Is your poem seaworthy? Does your poem float? Does it keep the water out? Does it have a kitchen? A place in which you can rest? Is it equipped with navigational tools? Can it withstand all kinds of weather? Do you trust it?

For me, the craft, the skill of writing falls into 3 categories; reading, playing and writing, writing being the least important of the 3. I'd also like to add have something to say, write beyond your abilities and be fearless. Wallace Stevens once said that the act of writing poetry was actually a very intense form of reading. If you want to write, you have to read. And read everything. Read the classic poets. Read contemporary poetry. Read journals, magazines, e-zines. If you find a poem you like, find everything that author has written and read it. Read fiction. Read biographies. Find out how the writers you love lived. It always makes me happy to read how neurotic most of the famous poets were. Read cookbooks, magazines, the operating instructions for small household appliances. Read advertisements on buses. Read your cereal box. Take notes.

Carry a notebook with you all the time. Sure, you're young now and you can remember a word that sparks you for at least a couple of weeks, but trust me, as you get older and your brain fills up, you'll be glad you have paper and pen on hand when you read the words pig trotters on a menu in a restaurant. It might take months before pig trotters actually find their way into a poem, but those words will be there, waiting for you when you need them. Create your own lexicon. Steal conversations. Write them down word for word. Sure, it makes people uncomfortable and they might suspect that you're writing down their conversation word for word but don't worry about that. We all have a desire to be immortalized in print. When you read, pay attention to what moves you, what works, what doesn't work. Read all the poetry you can find. And read the poetry you love as though you are writing it. If you find a poem you really love, memorize it. This will make it easier to steal from later.

The next point I want to talk about is play. I approach all art from a place of deep play. I think it is a mistake to take ourselves too seriously as artists. I'm not saying we shouldn't write about serious themes, we should. We should write about everything. What I am saying is that we should never forget why we write, we should never lose track of that goofy, glittery, fiery, child-like sense of wonder that made us want to do this odd thing in the first place. When you set out to write a poem, don't try to write something important. Poems that try to be important or intense or didactic most often fail. They lose sight of the human. I mean, we're funny. And the more tragic and heartbreaking our lives become, the funnier we get. Never lose track of that in your writing. I think art should celebrate the human condition, what ever it may be. Don't be afraid to take chances, to know nothing, to write from the beginner's mind, to invent everything brand new each time you sit down to write. Be honest in your writing. Be human.

The last thing I want to mention is writing. Sure, it seems obvious, but I'm not talking about writing when the fire is inside of you and everything is spilling out in a glorious outpouring. That's the easy part. The skill of crafting poetry lies in the revision, the cutting, the paring, the sweat. Richard Tillinghast, in an essay titled "Notes on Revision" says that "The willingness, the ardent desire even, to revise, separates the poet from the person who sees poetry as therapy or self-expression." Revision is the poet's most demanding, difficult and dangerous work. But I'm not going to talk about revision here because that would use at least five hours of my fifteen minutes. I want to talk about the practice of writing. Writing every day. I don't mean write a poem a day. But write something every day. Keep a daily journal. Take notes. Write letters.

I'm a violinist and I have to practice. I practice scales. I practice Mozart, sure, but it is the daily habit of practicing scales that allows me to play Mozart. Practicing scales every day allows me to stop thinking when I actually sit down to play Mozart. My brain can get out of the way and my body takes over. My fingers know where to go. This is where joy lies, for me, in the letting go. Is writing every day going to make the crafting of poetry easier? It might and it might not. But I can guarantee that once you get used to facing a blank page or the blue hum of a computer monitor every single day, that task becomes less daunting as time goes by. It gets easier to start. Your hand and your brain are used to this ritual. Fear is displaced by habit.

Rebecca Loudon lives and writes on Camano Island. She is the author of three collections of poetry, *Tarantella, Radish King*, and *Cadaver Dogs*, and two chapbooks, *Navigate, Amelia Earhat's Letters Home*, and *TRISM*.

The Paradox of Craft

Linda Clifton

February 12, 2004

...by indirection find direction out
                    —Hamlet

It's old news at this point in our history as readers and writers, the notion that our news comes to us in weasel words. We're so used to being manipulated that when, fewer than 24 hours after the twin towers came down on 9/11 and the major news networks assaulted us with headlines screaming "America at War," we didn't protest this twisting of our perceptions that a great crime had been committed against us. We didn't shout, "You've redefined a monumental crime as a war. You've launched us, without our deliberations, without our consideration, on the road to a military confrontation rather than a judicial solution. And you've done it before we even have a clue who committed these murders."

Many of us protested the war. Few of us protested that swift corruption of language. Or perhaps I'm being too harsh. Perhaps we protested but our voices never reached the public's ears, dominated as they were by a struggle over the one choice held up for public scrutiny: the choice to fight or to refrain.

This degradation of the public use of language presents us as writers with the terrible problem that the very language we seek to use has been made so malleable it now feels flabby in our hands. If language lies to us constantly, how can we hope to use it truly? If the music of rhyme sells war and soap and the new lime cola, how can we reclaim it for our own visions?

But that's the paradox of rhyme, of rhythm, and of the full panoply of writerly technique. And that's the paradox I want to address in this craft lecture: the paradox of approaching by indirection the center of what we want and mean to say. I want to discuss, in Hamlet's words, how craft helps us "by indirection find direction out."

For me, this collapse of confidence that makes me feel my words have gone all flat and flabby begins with the familiar specter of the editor who whispers behind my ear that I'm only saying what has been said and said and said before. Beside her stand fear of self-revelation, shame, timidity, embarrassment, and even fear of my own potential power. In a class once I actually constructed a collage of her; this fierce bear who glared at me from a tangle of emotional vines. I constructed her and then ceremonially burned her. All of us found the ceremony of burning our editors wonderfully inspiriting. Once the fire dies down, however, we still have to write.

And the real problem with writing is this: How do we break through restraint and fear to accuracy? It's not the confessional I seek when I urge us to tell the truth, nor the polemic. Our words may finally be confessions or political, but our obligation, especially in this time when so much language creates only manipulative codes, is to tell it true and that means to tell it with as much accuracy as our eyes and our sense of words can create. Accuracy, then—seeing as clearly as we can and choosing the words that help our reader see.

How, then, can we break through to accuracy? That's the paradox of craft. Craft can push us past constructed meaning to genuine discovery, and that discovery is the accurate revelation we seek. Let me give you some examples from my experience as a writer and a teacher. Teaching high schoolers the sonnet, for example, if I wanted interesting poems from them, poems that went deeper than "moon" and "June" and "dove" and "love," I showed them the sonnet as a chessboard of rhythm and rhyme scheme. I made them list their line ends, rhymed properly for the sonnet's pattern, and then asked them to fill in the iambic pentameter lines which would end with the words they had chosen. Because their rhymes were chosen for sound rather than meaning, their apparently random choices led them to thoughts they might not otherwise have brought to consciousness. With similar success, in poetry workshops, I ask participants to choose words from a variety of word caches, list them vertically in an order that seemed to them "right," and then write a poem around that "spine" of words. In both exercises, the results were pieces that surprised and delighted the writers and their readers. People who never wrote found they could make words say interesting things they'd never thought to articulate for themselves before they played this silly game I'd asked them to fool around with.

In other words, playing with the structure of the poem in some way allowed their pens to discover what they didn't know they could say. If you read my journals, you'll see instances of poems emerging for me by the same indirection: a page of nonsense rhymes followed by a real first line of a poem, followed by the full draft of a poem later polished and published. One of my students later told me he was able in this exercise to write this first poem, because "if it was a stupid poem it was because you gave us these stupid rules, and it was your fault, not mine, if I didn't like it." (He did like it.)

More accomplished poets than I and my students play similar games with words. Ibn Gabirol, an amazingly skilled medieval poet, used Hebrew acrostics for his mystical poems. I imagine him writing, immersed in the problem of making his acrostics work, like mathematical puzzles, like clicking the edges of boxes into place. I imagine him plunging himself into this problem he'd set, creating in himself the sense of the mystical he celebrated in his complex lines. As each poem spanned the *alefbet*, I imagine it spanned for Ibn Gabirol the foundational elements of God's universe, and for us, insights into his vision of those elements.

Attention to craft helps us revise, to see again, this time more clearly, what we're straining to see. You know some of these techniques: eliminate repeated words; look at the flow of metaphoric language; write it short; write it long; write in two-line chunks, or four or six; write it backwards from the bottom up—I could go on. But perhaps an example will be useful.

One of my journals contains five versions of a poem about Paul Celan, each a revision based on one of these strategies, none quite finished yet. Here's the first draft, written from a photo in the biography of Celan I was reading at the time. You'll recognize the title half-borrowed from Ezra Pound.

One Petal on a Black Bough
                            —Paul Celan in Czernowitz, 1937

Glance turned back over his left shoulder,
hands shoved into heavy wool pockets
against February's chill, his eyebrow
cocked under his leather cap's raked brim,
this boy caught on the street of strangers
by a stranger's camera, could break hearts
with his aloof face.
Instead, his heart
will constrict, pressed by history into such
distortions they will press him to his death,
though he has years and years more
to live a struggle to cleanse his dearest love
of vicious usurpations. His dearest love:
not the mother who loved him, but the language
she taught him to love in her stillness and warmth,
her shaping of each syllable with her loving life's breath.

Next, I wrote it backwards. I started with the last line and worked up until I had to begin to change the sentence to create its sense, at which point the poem changed materially. I wrote beside it at the time: "inter-

esting—now it's her poem more than his. It gets somewhere different."
Here's a draft of this second version.

Two Petals

"the silence is no silence" Paul Celan, 1959

With her loving life's breath,
her warm shaping of syllables
she taught him to love, in its stillness,
not this mother who taught,
but her language,
their dearest love,
dearest, to be cleansed
as he lived on, years, years, pressed
under history, his heart constricting so
the blood hardly flowed through the temples
assaulted by wave after wave
of terrible power erasing
memory,
sound,
the shapes
of words
but never
this void
edged
by crackling
smoke.

All the revisions that followed brought me closer to seeing Celan,
his journey through the pain of the Holocaust, and his poems, to an
understanding that I had been seeking when I chose to read the book.
Craft brought me closer to understanding. And trying yet another strategy—write it short—shaped the poem in shorter lines, more elusive lan-

guage in this last version, and it became a memorial poem, a "yiskor" or "memorial prayer"—nearer completion though not quite ready to leave the drafting table.

Yizkor

"the silence is no silence" Paul Celan, 1959

With her breath's
warm shape of syllables
she taught him to love
in its stillness
the mother/ her
language
dearest
dearest to be scoured
pure as he lived
years
years
heart constricting so
blood hardly flowed
through the temples
assaulted
wave after
wave
erasing memory
sound
the shapes of words
but never
this void
edged by
whispering
smoke.

Whether I'm closer to the poem I'm trying to write or not, I felt with each revision closer to understanding this difficult poet I've been struggling to know. How did my attention to craft as a prompt for revision work to bring me closer? Craft gives us pleasure that distracts us productively from the need to be "right" and "important." Craft enters the picture whether we use strict form, like Ibn Gabirol or Richard Wilbur, or looser, freer verse. I remember writing a piece in free verse, a very political poem, about the war in El Salvador; what powered that poem to completion, even more than my revulsion at the war itself, was fascination with placing the line breaks so that the poem would readexactly as my mind's ear heard it. Why line breaks? Because I'd just been in a workshop with Denise Levertov in which she laid out her theory about how line breaks instruct the reader to use the voice. The pleasure intensified when I gave the poem to a friend who is a professional actor and he read it just as I heard it in my head, guided only by the marks on the page. (He liked the politics too.)

Craft, then, lets us keep our eye on the problem, not on the fact that we are "writing a poem" nor on the poem's idea. Craft keeps our focus on potential rather than intended meaning. It can move us past intent to discovery. But craft can only do this if we remember one more rule, the rule I keep secret from my students until they've really wrestled to the point of frustration with the strictures of craft. (The freest of my students discover the secret rule on their own.) Shakespeare remembers this secret every time the true rhythm of his sonnet moves against its strict iambics. The secret rule: "Break the rules and make the poem."

I began this talk with an indictment of manipulated language, language used to make us conform as citizens. Such language cares nothing about truth but a great deal about concealment. In contrast, craft's adherence to form makes us look at ideas "slant," as Emily Dickinson wrote, helps us move past inhibition to insight, and, if we break its rules to make the poem, moves us closer to truth.

Linda Clifton founded *Crab Creek Review* in 1983 & edited the magazine for 12 years. She was guest editor in Aug. 1999 of *The Hedgebrook Journal*. Her poetry has appeared in *Calyx*, & other small magazines. She earned a PhD in medieval literature at the University of Washington. A former K-12 Director of the Puget Sound Writing Project at UW, she led teacher workshops on poetry, on teaching writing and on Washington State educational assessments of writing. A teacher of high school literature & writing, she retired after 34 years, the last 14 in Northshore School District. She now offers editorial services to private clients.

Some Things I've Thought About and Observed About Not Writing and Writing

Sheila Bender

November 11, 2004

Part I: Let Your Writer Self Be With You

"Issues of productivity," "sitting still with loneliness and boredom," "compartments of time." I mulled these phrases over. A close writing colleague was suffering from writer's block and had written them to me in a letter. As I thought about what I consider the source of writer's block, I dialed my cousin. I often make phone calls while I am thinking about things that I don't have answers for.

She was busy—"I have twelve cakes in the oven," she said, "Can you believe it? In addition, her two single young adult children were visiting from other cities, and needing to move, she was looking for a new apartment. Wow, I thought, that's a lot.

Then I considered my husband, who was busy writing two articles at once for a technical journal. He had taken me to a movie the evening before because he couldn't get anywhere in his writing. Mulling over both my husband and my cousin's projects, I realized something about my own approach to creating. I had made six kinds of soup from scratch in the last two weeks since I started teaching several days a week because I need to do something while I worry about what I will say to my students.

Each of us bakes our creative cakes so differently. My husband walks away from the cakes, hoping that once he is away from them, they'll continue to cook somewhere deep inside of him. Sure enough, after we'd eaten a quick teriyaki meal and drunk a cup of coffee and taken our seats in the theater, the "aha hit." Not only did he know what was at the root of his articles' problems, he realized his new understanding meant he wouldn't have to start over. Boy, he enjoyed that movie! But he would have anyway, even if the "aha" was delayed. He counts on it arriving sometime. There's always HBO waiting at home until the moment strikes.

My cousin—well her cakes are for real—she's a health food chef and teacher and an allergy free dessert specialist. She'll keep right on putting those babies in and out of the oven and publishing her recipes in *Vegetarian Times*. Sometimes she makes mistakes that lead to treasured discoveries. Recently, when she reached for rice cereal instead of flour, she decided to bake the cake using it! Later, she watched her guests put their first forkfuls into their mouths. They thought the cake was delicious and she had a new wheat-free dessert.

I group things. I was teaching so the writing was on the back burner and I got into my domestic chores between classes. After the quarter, when the courses were done for a stretch, I'd be writing up a storm, the frozen food I'd stored in my freezer decreasing daily.

I am a user of "compartments of time," but my cousin and my husband use "currents of time" and notice the little surprises that bob up and down in them.

I don't know, if you are like them or me or someone else, dear reader, but let me propose something for those of you who need to get over writer's block, severe or mild. My suggestion comes from reading *Who's Writing This?* edited by *Anteaus* literary magazine editor Daniel Halpern. It is a collection of essays by 50 writers and poets on writing and writers block published by The Ecco Press in 1994. Halpern had entreated contributors to respond to Jorge Luis Borges' statement, "It is to my other self, to Borges, that things happen."

Reading this, I began to imagine the writer in me as a separate being from the me who has been going, doing, bitching, wishing to own things and making plans. If Bender is my self to whom things happen, then maybe my writing voice, which is the self to whom things don't happen, has some nice insight as an observer on what is happening to Bender and whatever it is that distracts her from the writer's work and voice.

But how does this writer person, the one to whom things have not happened, the one that doesn't have cakes in the oven, the one who chooses the batter of the written word over and over again, get through to me, the one who owns the computer?

I continued mulling this over for a few days as I taught and did chores. When my husband again asked me to go see a movie, I said no because I was going to make soup. While I chopped, I found that the rhythm of chopping all those vegetables occupied the Bender to whom things happen and made the writer inside of her, the one to whom things do not happen, think about things. She was remembering a lot. She remembered events like the time her mother cut a finger badly just as her dad came home from a week on the road as a traveling salesman and planting a vegetable garden one summer. She remembered her son's quails laying eggs in a cage just to the side of the garden. The one to whom things does not happen remembered the way Bender's husband buys beets of many colors and roasts them in the oven. She thought of the way Bender's daughter stuffs artichokes with cloves of garlic and puts lemon juice in the pot of water she boils them in, thereby refining a family delight. As Bender chopped vegetables, the one to whom things do not happen was chopping the events of Bender's life into images that delight or concern or make Bender cry. She thought of the day the quail were eaten by a raccoon and a friend said, "Of course, they were helpless prey, unable to escape the cage." She thought of how she could use this newly surfaced thought to write about something important to find out about, something about how what nourished Bender's son with its eggs and beauty was lost because it was captive to a family that didn't know how to protect it. She will learn how much sorrow Bender holds knowing this is true for so much besides the quail of long ago. As the soup simmered, she was writing.

My idea is that if or when you experience a writing block, you will adopt a rhythmic action like running, shooting baskets, cooking, dancing, swimming, or bicycle riding and let the writer in you separate from your life's doings and burst into words! As you concentrate on what you are doing, the one inside to whom things do not happen, the writing and observing person, will find that images surface. If the one who is doing allows the images to register, that one who is doing will sit down and let the one who is writing write!

Part II: Commit to pushing through the prickly leaves of doubt and keep on writing

My grandson Toby turned 17 months old this October 1. He has been talking for months and he loves words. "All done Mommy phone," he says when my daughter Emily is talking with me and he wants her full attention. "All done Mommy bed," he says when he wants her to wake up in the morning. "All done elephants," he says when he is at the zoo and ready to move on to the hippopotamuses. His mom taught him sign language for this phrase very early and he has been communicating with it for quite awhile. At first, the gesture she taught him, which requires lifting and shaking both hands, proved most wonderful as an expedient way to be sure he didn't touch the soiled area of his diaper when she was removing it. "All done, Toby," she'd say, "We're all done with your dirty diaper," and Toby would shake his hands while Emily quickly pulled the dirty diaper away from his body, happy to have kept him talking with his fingers so he couldn't put them into the mess.

Soon, he was signing "all done" when he didn't want any more food or when he was tired of sitting in a lap or when his interest in looking at a particular book expired. And not long after that, he was saying, "All done."

One evening, when he was 14 months old, I took him outside his parents' third story apartment to play with the toy car they kept parked under the apartment building stairwell so his mommy could cook without interruption. He could hear her chopping through the open window, and he looked up from the courtyard toward the window. "All done. Mommy. All done. Mommy," he chanted, communicating to his grandma that he most certainly did not want to be outside another second without his mommy.

Not wanting to fail in my mission of occupying Toby for a little bit, I suggested that we look for a rock for Mommy. Toby's eyes lit up. We walked around and around the raised beds of the landscaped courtyard, but we couldn't find a rock. As we walked to the next building, Toby looked back toward his mommy's window and then reluctantly continued the search. When I spied a solitary rock, I balanced Toby on the ledge of the masonry bed that held several shrubs, a tree and flowers, and held onto him as I pointed to the rock. He eagerly reached for it, but he managed to put his hand on a shrub that had prickly thorns at the end of each leaf. He burst into tears. I kissed that hand and reached for the rock myself. "All done," I said, no longer wanting to keep him away from the woman who lit up his life. "Let's go see Mommy."

When we came in the door, Toby toddled over to his mom and held out the rock.
"Thank you," Emily said. "Is that for Mommy? Let's put it up here on the bookshelf."

The rock was more than a gift. It carried Toby's feelings about being apart from Emily. Received by her, the rock healed the small wound. The world was right again.

As writers, we are in the position of being outside looking up at a window behind which those we love are busy. We want to hang around with them and tell them our deepest truest perceptions and feelings, but they often need for us not to talk so intimately. And so we go into exile for a little while to write our stories and poems, to share our impressions, yearnings, and discoveries. If we are lucky, we find the rock—the subject of our writing or the form that allows us to say what we need to. However, reaching for the words, we may lose our balance and fall into prickly plants. Then we must keep on writing; we must call up the lessons of writers who have been our teachers. We must stay immersed in the process of writing. If we do, a force greater than ourselves seems to pull the rock toward us or even hands it to us.

When people in the world, even people quite different than those we thought we were writing for, accept our gift, they also accept our sadness at having to be apart from the world that we love in order to write about it. And for the moment we are home and can say, "All done sadness." And then more perceptions come and we will write our way into and out of exile, again and again.

Those of us compelled to write, understand these lines by the poet Theodore Roethke in "The Waking": "This shaking keeps me steady. I should know." We understand what poet Philip Levine meant when he said, "Why do I write? Because I don't feel well if I don't."

When you feel the prickly leaves of doubt hurting your confidence in authoring, remember these words from Lorca, "As for me, I can explain nothing, but stammer with the fire that burns inside me, and the life that has been bestowed on me." Then keep writing from direct experience. Don't worry about what the head wants to puzzle out—report your experience through your senses. Write down what you heard, saw, touched, tasted and smelled. Before you know it, you will be absorbed in writing the experience, rather than explaining it. You will be putting fire on the page.

When you feel the prickly leaves of grief pulled up by your words, remember Ring Lardner said, "How can you write if you can't cry?" Write through your tears. There will come a time in the process when you are so at one that your tears dry. And when you have written the full experience of your grief, you will feel peace. When grief resides on the page, its residence is love.

When you feel the prickly leaves of fear because you cannot control your writing but must abandon yourself to what you have called up, think about Toby's rock, about the gift you are making. Imagine even one person receiving it, feeling thanks for it, and placing it among their treasured things.

When you feel the prickly leaves of distress at saying the truth and imagining others hearing you say it, remember writer Rita Mae Brown's words, "Writers are the moral purifiers of the culture. We may not be pure ourselves, but we must tell the truth, which is a purifying act." Write what you have in you to write. You can decide later what to do about those for whom this writing would not be a gift. Many times you will be surprised when the work is finished. Those you were most afraid would shun the work, may love it.

When you feel the prickly leaves of thinking you never have enough time to write because writing requires a special mood, write something down—any thought or image will do. Soon you will notice that you have five minutes to write, then ten minutes and then you will find twenty. You will have words to get back to if you write something down. You will gain dexterity in altering your state of being to the writing state. You will begin to work on the projects you have inside yourself. Your practice will be writing rather than wishing you were writing. You might find yourself chanting, "All done not writing. All done."

Sheila Bender's most recent book is: *Writing Personal Essays: Shaping and Sharing Your Life Experience.* Her other recently reprinted instructional books include: *Writing in a Convertible with the Top Down* (co-authored with Christi Killien Glover) *and Sorrow's Words: Writing Exercises to Heal*

Grief. Sheila's books also include her recent poetry collection *Behind Us the Way Grows Wider* and her memoir *A New Theology: Turning to Poetry in a Time of Grief*. She is founder of WritingItReal.com, a site dedicated to helping those who write from personal experience in poems, essays, memoir, journals and fiction. As a student of David Wagner, she took his advice seriously: if you are a poet you must always learn to write in another genre, too. Sheila is a graduate of the University of Washington with an MA in Creative Writing. She teaches at writers' workshops in the western US and conducts online workshops and tutorials. She has served as Distinguished Guest Lecturer at Seattle University.

Tracking Your Poetry Submissions

Michael Dylan Welch

December 9, 2004 (updated February 2019)

Just as an actor needs a stage, a poet needs to publish. Yet how can poets keep track of their submissions in an inexpensive and orderly way? Computer databases offer help with this task, and *Submittable* and other online tools offer efficient ways to submit and track your submissions, but I use a system that I started before I had a computer—and still prefer it. I write the poem's title or the entire poem (if short enough) on a 4-by-6-inch index card and add the places and dates of submission and response. It's easy to keep track of submissions using these cards, and I can easily shuffle the cards as I decide what to send where, or to sequence them. Because the system is straightforward and uninhibiting, it encourages me to send out my work for publication. Perhaps this system might work for you.

Why keep good records of your poetry submissions?
You avoid repeating a submission—or control or prevent simultaneous submissions.
You keep from submitting previously published work (the more you publish, the more often this is likely to happen).
You can collect publication data for résumé or bibliographical purposes.
What to track on index cards when submitting your poetry:
Poem (write the poem on the card if short enough or keep an alphabetical or numerical master file in a binder or in a computer file that corresponds to your submission cards by title or first line).
Date(s) and place(s) when you wrote/revised the poem, plus notes on composition.

Place submitted (also note how much you spend on entry fees or reading fees, if any):

    Journal (note whether it's print or online)

    Anthology

    Contest

Date submitted.

Date response received (you can track how long a response takes with dates):

    "ACCEPTED" (I like to put this is capital letters as a small personal celebration); if submitted for a contest, I write "WON" and state the placement

    "Returned" (one need not use the term "Rejected")

If accepted for a journal or anthology, note the following for later bibliographic reference:

    The publication's full title

    Expected volume/issue/date (usually specified by the editor)

    Editor's name (handy to have for future correspondence)

    Page number (when a copy is received)

    Payment ($ or copies, if any)

    Rights you offered or the editor acquired (if different from one-time serial rights)

If the work places in a contest, note the following:

    Name(s) of contest judge(s)

    Name of prize won (and $ amount, if any)

    Expected name/date/publisher of publication (if any)

Include other miscellaneous notes, such as whether an editor offered comments, or if he or she was helpful, professional, abrasive, or whatever, if you're asked to resubmit or make a particular revision, or whether the poem appeared with typos. You may also want to keep track of any contracts and proofs (dates received and sent).

Arrangement of index card boxes (separate boxes for each category):
Poems ready for submission (in no particular order).

Poems assigned to journals, awaiting submission (awaiting deadlines or my having time to submit).

Poems currently out for consideration (grouped by publication or contest).

Poems accepted but not yet published (grouped by publication or contest).

Poems that have been published (arranged alphabetically by title or first line); some of these cards go back into box 2 and then box 3 if requested for publication elsewhere, such as in anthologies, or if submitted elsewhere if the publication allows prior publication.

You could also keep another card file for publication addresses, noting when you subscribed or when you need to renew. Other systems are possible to track your poetry submissions, especially online and using database systems on your computer, but this system works for me. Perhaps it will work for you! Whatever system you use, the principles and data referred to here should apply to other systems as well.

Resources to use for making submissions:

Poet's Market, published annually by Writer's Digest Books (http://www.writersdigest.com/).

Little Magazines & Small Presses and Directory of Poetry Publishers, each published annually by *Dustbooks* (http://www.dustbooks.com/).

Start with local magazines, such as ones available in local bookstores (read your local journals!).

Michael Dylan Welch has served two terms as poet laureate of Redmond, Washington, curates readings for SoulFood Poetry Night and the Redmond Association of Spokenword, and directs the Poets in the Park festival. He also runs National Haiku Writing Month (NaHaiWriMo.com). In 2012, one of his translations (with Emiko Miyashita) appeared on the back of 150,000,000 U.S. postage stamps, and in 2013 he was keynote speaker at the Haiku International Association conference in Tokyo. Michael lives with his wife and two children in Sammamish,

Washington. His latest books include *Seven Suns / Seven Moons* (with Tanya McDonald), *Off the Beaten Track*, *Fire in the Treetops*, and *Becoming a Haiku Poet*. His website, devoted mostly to haiku and other poetry, is Graceguts.com

Finding Your Subject

Peter Pereira

February 10th, 2005

I was asked recently to speak to a college poetry class about "Finding Your Subject." All writers, but particularly younger or beginning writers, struggle with the feeling of wanting to write, but not knowing what to write about. The well-worn advice of "write what you know," "write about what's important to you," "write the poem/story you would like to read," "write about what you are afraid to write about," these are all good and valid ways to cast about and find a subject.

In my own writing, I find my subject in many different spheres of experience: from my work as a doctor in a community clinic; from my own family history; from travel and the garden; from my long-term relationship with my partner of 18 years; from language itself, in word play and word games. But the more I thought about it, what seemed most true to me, and my experience as a writer, is that we don't necessarily find our subject, our subject finds us.

And your subject can find you at the most inconvenient times: Driving down the freeway in the snow, with no pen, no paper. At 2:00 am when you need to sleep because you have to work early the next day. At a birthday party for your sister, or a baptism for your niece. When the kids need a ride to the movies. When your partner wants to have "a talk." Always when you are least expecting it.

So it is important to be ready. To have prepared a welcoming place in your life, so when the subject that is out there finds you, it can come in, sit down, and stay a while. So how does one get ready? I think there are three important things you can do:

1) make a space in your life for reflection
2) do regular writing practice, as well as spur-of-the-moment note-making
3) learn to recognize the signs that a subject has found you

I'd like to talk with you a little bit about each one of these.

1) Make space in your life for reflection:

For me, it is important to have space and time for reflection in one's life. We all have such busy lives. We're plugged in to cell phones and pagers and email and voice messages. We're never really quiet. We drive with the radio on. We eat with the TV playing in the background. We don't get enough silence.

So I have chosen to work part-time, Monday, Wednesday, and Friday, so that I can have Tuesday and Thursday, and sometimes weekends, free for reflection, and to write. I try to cultivate periods of quiet into these days. I have nothing planned to do. I listen to music, wander the garden, walk in the park, hang out in the used bookstore, the coffee shop, go for a drive to the mountains. My partner has learned that even though it may look like I am not "doing anything," that sitting by myself in the window seat, staring out the window, simply regarding the sky, is writing. Cultivating this slowed-down, reflective, openness to the world, for whatever thoughts rise up and fall away, rise up and fall away, prepares you for being ready, so that the subject, like a timid little bird, will some days quietly light into the palm of your hand. Cultivating this slowed-down, reflective, openness to the world creates a kind of life rhythm, so that the subject that is out there, looking for you, begins to learn how to reach you, learns your patterns, your proclivities, and when is the best time to get your attention.

2) Do regular writing practice, as well as spur-of-the-moment note-making:

I try to carry paper and pen with me always; and this has been made much easier with the emergence of the PDA. This is so I can jot down quickly the whispers and phrases and glimmerings that are often the first signs that a subject is trying to find me. I keep a tiny notebook at my bedside, with a pen and a little flashlight, so if there is a voice in my head as I am falling asleep, or just as I am waking up, I can jot down what it says, because this is often an important message from the subject that is trying to find me.

For my regular writing practice, I keep a journal, and a notebook. The journal is written on my laptop, and then printed on sticky paper that I place in a hardbound book. In it I write about fairly mundane things: the weather, what happened at work yesterday, what I am doing with my partner for his birthday, etc. This journal is not usually a place where my subject finds me, though sometimes it sneaks in that way. My journal is really more a form of writing practice, getting words and sentences down onto paper, in a way that makes sense, with grammar and punctuation and order. It's a way of getting into the rhythm of writing about what is going on in my daily life, a sort of official record of "what happened," but not at a very deep level. It is a way to get out all that chit-chat language in your head that is like white noise, or radio interference, preventing your subject from tuning into you.

After writing in my journal for a while, I close the laptop and turn to my notebook. This is a five-subject spiral-ring, with pockets for newspaper clippings, articles, post-it notes, and other debris. I write with a pen: notes, phrases, images, lines, sometimes just single words that I can go back to later, and mine for poems. This is where I collect some of the random jottings collected from the previous days or weeks. And put them to paper, to see if anything coheres. I do a lot of free writing and doodling in my notebook. And when the subject has found me, this is where the poem begins.

3) Learn to recognize the signs that a subject has found you:

How do you know when your subject how found you? For me it is a physical sense. An urgency. Perhaps what I imagine a woman might feel when she is about to go into labor? Or what an epileptic might feel when he is about to have a seizure? It's a EUREKA! kind of feeling, an overwhelming sense that there is a voice and a rhythm and a purpose that is needing to be written, to be said. That there is a poem in me, and the writing of it just flows out. I may have no idea where the poem is headed, and then discover it as the writing proceeds. I'll fill several pages before I stop. It is usually not difficult writing. In fact, it is perhaps the easiest part of writing (revision being a very different beast, is much harder work; but that's another lecture). This "flow" phase is perhaps the most satisfying part of writing; because you have prepared yourself, and made a ready space in your life, and your subject has arrived, and you are ready to receive it.

[Re-printed at *Good Times*, a Santa Cruz County News and Entertainment Weekly.]

Peter Pereira is a family physician in Seattle, and an editor at Floating Bridge Press, which he co-founded in 1994. Many of his poems arise from his medical practice, and have appeared in *Poetry, Prairie Schooner, The Virginia Quarterly Review, Journal of the American Medical Association*, and elsewhere. Winner of the 1997 "Discovery"/The Nation Award, his books include *The Lost Twin* (Grey Spider 2000) and *Saying the World* (Copper Canyon 2003) which won the Hayden Carruth Award, and was a finalist for the Lambda Literary Award, the Triangle Publishing Award, and the PEN USA Award in Poetry.

Pam's Prose Practicum

Pamela Moore Dionne

March 10, 2005

Writing is an odd and solitary practice, at least when a writer is actually at the keyboard blackening a page with what she believes is the story or poem that will take her somewhere worthwhile. If you're interested in writing you should plan to spend huge amounts of time sitting on your butt hunched over a keyboard with your shoulders rolled forward into what will someday be a permanent posture. Another little bonus you can expect to accompany the craft of writing (and which is directly related to all that time spent in front of a keyboard) is that the afore-mentioned butt is going to spread until ultimately it mimics the size and shape of the chair cushion on which the writer sits while punching out her opus.

Believe it or not, this is a pretty standard way to hone craft. It's the nec-essary daily grind. You put in your chair jockey time to practice your instrument. This is what teaches you how to problem solve with your characters when you've written them into a corner, which you will do on a pretty regular basis. This is where and how you'll learn to trust your characters to tell their story so that all you have to do is get out of the way and take dictation.

I write poetry and fiction, as well as a little nonfiction when pressed. In each of these disciplines, my focus is almost always character. I believe that once you develop a fully realized character, your story or your poem takes on its own life and you're set free to write what you witness unfold-ing in that world, taking on flesh, bone, shoe leather and concrete inside your imagination.

You can read all the how-to books on writing that you want and they'll give you some pretty good advice. They'll also give you completely useless information that works great for the writer who authored a particular tome on writing but won't do a thing for you as a writer trying to learn your craft or, for that matter, as a writer trying to improve your craft. So, before I begin to lay this one out for you, I guess I feel compelled to give you a caveat, a cautionary notice that goes something like "reader/listener—beware."

I'm about to give you writing advice that may or may not be helpful, that may or may not make any sense at all given your personality, gender, age, political bent, philosophical leanings, work ethic, current health status, sexual preference, etc." Basically any variable you want to insert will make an apt disclaimer. It's my belief that all advice should come with such a disclaimer.

And so let's begin with Pam's Prose Practicum:

Here's a plot for you: Pearl Boggs is a white woman in her 80's who leaves her husband of 71 years and takes up with a black man she meets during her travels. Not very interesting, yet, you say.

Okay, let's try this: Pearl Boggs is 87 years old, married 71 of those years to a man who decades earlier drank himself blind with his own corn liquor mash. What Pearl and Old Bob don't know is that Pearl is about to leave her home in Ash Flat, Arkansas. Not only that, she's about to leave Old Bob and strike out on her own hitchhiking across America where she will meet Maitland Pruitt, an 85-year-old retired Baptist minister and widower.

Maitland is a black man who dislikes most whites on principle but especially dislikes uneducated rednecks, which is how he sums up Pearl on their first meeting. Maitland becomes entangled with Pearl when he mistakenly believes he has compromised her sexually. He can't think of a reasonable way to extricate himself from her, so this misunderstanding keeps the two travelers together long enough to give them time to discover what each inherently has to offer the other.

These are both renderings of the same story plot. It is in fact the plot of a story I wrote which was published some time ago. The difference between these two versions is fairly simple to explain. The first version has no life, no breath, and no reality. In the second version, characters begin to develop as personalities who come from real places where they live with real family members. One of these narrative descriptions gives very little detail, the other gives very specific information.

The point is details are what make characters come to life. To develop these characters into a full-blown story, I can give one of them a distinctive walk; another may have a mannerism that could be easily inserted into the text of a story without becoming irritating or repetitive. Each of them might have unique ways of phrasing things that would make dialogue easier to identify and follow. They have different levels of education, different levels of practical wisdom, different ways of seeing the world and their place in that world. In other words, these characters have histories because they've lived lives. And it's the small details of these histories that I, as an author, will sift through and use within the context of the story I'm telling.

How do I find these historical details for fictional characters, you ask.

I do my homework. Once I've become enamored with a character or characters, I set the narrative in a real time period. Knowing when and where my characters live gives me the opportunity to find the headlines that would have mattered to them and would have figured into the personal history of the character.

I give my characters actual birthdates and read their horoscopes for clues to personality. I know where each character was born, where and how each was raised, what they were educated to be and where they were educated, what traumas they suffered, what joys. Basically I interview them to find out every little detail that might be usable.

Then, when I feel I'm acquainted with each character, I let them walk through my imagination with the story they want to tell me. I no longer attempt to have a story plotted out in advance, because my characters always ignore that script and write their own. And I find it's more interesting for me to write this way than to follow some formula from beginning to end. I think I'd actually be incapable of sticking around to write the end of something if I knew exactly what that end was going to be. This might be very different for genre writers, but since I don't write genre, knowing my precise plot in advance is not a requirement.

My approach to the craft of writing allows me to be surprised by my characters. It keeps me open to plot twists that might not otherwise occur if I were more controlling about the process. It keeps my writing fresh and varied. But most importantly, it forces me to be more attentive to character. If a character has not been fully realized, it won't be capable of leading a writer anywhere. That means the story will cease to progress. It'll die on the page. Or, and this is perhaps the worst scenario, it will continue in a formulaic pattern to a predictable end. This is the antithesis of good writing. Don't go there.

What you as a writer may want to take away from this presentation is that there are many ways to approach craft. None is an absolute. The craft of writing is as individual as each of us who writes. One writer will tell you that you must write every day. Perhaps she will even recommend that you write every day at the same time for the same length of time. This would be too confining for me.

A good writer needs to live life in a world where she encounters other human beings. These are the characters that will ultimately people your plots. Without experience, life is dull. This same thing can and should be said for writing. Experience will feed your imagination. It will give you an ear for the voices that begin to emerge in your writing as a natural process of having become aware of the inflections in the world around you.

Part of writing is living your life and paying attention while you're doing that living. Eavesdrop in cafes, on the street, in elevators. Listen for the way speakers string words together. Listen to regional accents. Become a mimic.

Don't stop there. Go skydiving or terrify yourself in some other way and live through it. I guarantee that whatever exhilaration you wrench from this life will worm its way into your writing some day when you least expect it and enrich a scene that might otherwise have fallen flat.

A writer is a storyteller. Good storytellers spend time in the world where stories occur. Later they go home and embellish what they've seen, heard, felt, or experienced. Hemmingway and Anaïs Nin come to mind as good examples for this writing-what-you-live kind of approach.

So my advice on craft pretty much boils down to: Go out into the world, pay attention to the people you meet, take notes ask questions and listen to the answers. This will serve you well when you begin interviewing your characters. Be prepared to borrow from the real people you meet in order to create your fictional characters. Pay attention to the news of the day so that you can use it as anchoring for your fictional plot.

Once you've got your characters and a timeframe, research the history for your characters' personal passage through time. Use some of those headlines you found in order to mesh fiction with fact. Create character studies that function like a memory of someone you actually know in reality. This is what will make your characters real.

Now, let your characters tell their story. Don't get in the way. Be attentive and follow along typing as they dictate. Call them on it when something rings false but keep writing. It may be that another character is meant to expose this untruth within the unfolding story and what you have to do is trust in the process. Keep writing till you come to the end of the tale. Keep writing even if all of your poems or stories end up in a dresser drawer never to be published in your lifetime. It worked for Emily Dickenson.

That's all I've got to give you on the craft of writing. I hope some of it helps.

Pamela Moore Dionne was the founder and managing editor of *Literary Salt*, which was an art and literary journal. Her poetry and fiction can be found in print and online journals. Dionne has been a Jack Straw Writer and a poet in residence at Centrum. She received both a Jack Straw AAP Grant and an Artist Trust GAP Grant. Currently she is working on her MFAW at Goddard College.

Filling More Than the Page

David Massengill

April 13, 2006

Three years ago, I quit fiction writing. I was 28, and I'd just completed *News on Frances Connelly*, a short story collection about my hometown in the Bay Area. I'd envisioned the manuscript as my first publishable project, yet I wasn't receiving any rewards for my work. Though past tales of mine had appeared in literary magazines, I'd failed to place a single one of these stories in any publication—a necessary feat if I wanted to gain a publisher for the collection. Being an artsy, financially struggling city dweller, I was exhausted with the book's subject matter of insular, upper-class, suburban society, and I had no drive to revise or add stories. How could I accompany another middle-aged homemaker heroine through the process of revelation when I myself was stuck in life? I'd been diligently crafting short stories for nearly 10 years, and during that entire time I'd made less money off my fiction than I did working at my current day job for a month.

So why, I brooded, should I continue to write? I stepped back from the keyboard and stopped sending my manuscript to literary agents. And I signed up for a painting class. Now I recognize my turning from type to brushstroke as a regression to my childhood. I'd adored drawing as a boy, and the cartoons and comics I produced earned me instant praise. For a short while, painting brought my adult self joy. I discovered a quick sort of therapy through working with colors instead of words, and I appreciated how the impact of a painting arrives with one glance rather than minutes or hours of reading and thinking.

But I missed fiction writing to my core, and though my tales no longer appeared on page they multiplied in my mind—whenever I followed the storyline of another's novella or horror movie or pop song, and each time a friend talked of a neurosis or epiphany. I had characters in my skull banging to leave, and I suspected it was vital to release them if I wanted to maintain my own sense of liberty.

I started writing fiction again, less than three months after I'd stopped. As I began, I hoisted some guidelines so I wouldn't slip back into that pit of misery with my writing. I'd like to share these six guidelines with you tonight, not because I view them as absolutes or because I think they should replace yours. I'm revealing my guidelines because they may help some of you continue writing when such an act seems impossible.

1. Write for the sake of writing (and not for any loot).

If your primary purpose in writing fiction is to earn money or get published, you should either practice something more lucrative—like technical writing or law—or know that you're heading toward regret. Sure, you may receive checks for your work, and you may have your name appear in literary magazines or along the spine of a book. But the chances of financial success are few and the rejection letters and years of dejection can be many. However, if you write because you love the creative process or you want to advance your capabilities or expression brings you peace, then you have a sturdy mindset for being a fiction writer.

When I was battling my own writing-related disillusionment, I signed up for a class called "Intuitive Writing" at the University of Washington's Experimental College. Concerned with enabling students how to ignore their internal critics and create in spontaneous and unconventional ways, the class was a catalyst for many inspirations. I recall asking the instructor at the start of the course if she ever mailed her poems to journals. "I don't send them out," she said without a hint of bitterness. "I write them for myself." I couldn't fathom why she neglected this normal striving for recognition until I witnessed how much happiness she achieved from birthing a work of verse. Now I know it is essential to write for oneself first, and others second. If an audience builds then these readers are perks for your fiction, and not its impetus.

2. Write what you want to know, not just what you know

I've always resented the "write what you know" motto emphasized in creative writing manuals and workshops. Of course, your fiction will have more force if you write with authority. But the insistence that creative writers write only about what they've experienced can cause censorship of the imagination, and the fear of writing outside one's own category of age, race, gender, sexuality, or lifespan. If you're a 23-year-old Argentinean woman who's familiar with kleptomania then you'll be fine writing about Roman soldiers pillaging a Celtic village in 23 B.C. Fiction writing is not reporting, nor is it memoir. You can write about what you've never seen and whom you've never met, and Oprah will never crucify you for embellishing.

I used to obey the unofficial law of "write what you know," which kept my fiction within the boundaries of contemporary realism. More recently, I've penned stories about Frida Kahlo's dreamtime, a gay couple in 1938 Nazi Munich, and medieval unicorn hunters. Each journey I take to another time or continent or reality brings me delight and enlightenment. I've noticed that my best fiction comes from my writing the tales I want to read, even if those tales are beyond my domain of direct knowledge. What we all know and what we all share is human consciousness, so we should rove across this terrain as much as we dare.

3. Listen to yourself more than others

I believe that each of us possesses an intuitive voice that can communicate what will nourish us and what will cause us to be sick. I interpret this to be the voice of one's truest and most honorable self, the self that thinks in terms of wellbeing and growth rather than wealth and celebrity. We sometimes ignore this voice because it seems as irrational and unfashionable as the kooky person on the sidewalk whom everyone pretends not to hear. Our intuitive voice often directs us to write in an eccentric manner or create in ways we never have before. The intuitive voice is frequently in opposition to the voice of the ego as well as the voices of our peers, like book critics and graduates of MFA programs and whichever author placed a story in *The New Yorker* this week.

When I wrote my last story collection, I followed the literary logic of the times and constructed an easily digestible and non-experimental book on a little town mired in money. I had Sherwood Anderson's *Winesburg, Ohio* and the novels of Edith Wharton to support my choice in creation, as small societies and aristocrats have always been acceptable subject matter in the history of literary fiction. As I rebuilt after the crash related to this book, I desired to write something less ordinary: works of flash fiction. Also called short-shorts or microfiction, flash fiction is a short short story that usually combines the structure of an average-length story and the language of a poem. The genre is a bit of a redheaded stepchild, as many poets label it unpoetic prose poetry and many fiction writers call it sketching that should have stayed on a Post-It.

Two novelists in my writers group offered reluctant smiles upon reading some of my one-sentence to one-page stories and said, "These pieces are enjoyable, but they'll be so tough to publish. We think you'd write such a good novel." I heard their warning that my new work might meet rejection, yet my intuitive voice was crying for me to proceed with the flash fiction. And I did, which has led to the near completion of another collection. I don't know if the work will reach print, but I'm aware of the peak of satisfaction I attained by creating what my truest self wanted to create.

One further comment on listening to others: Criticism and compliments concerning your fiction are the same—worth a bit of your consideration, and then meant to dissipate. If there's something you truly need to improve in your writing, your intuitive voice will inform you.

4. Remember that you are a person before you are a writer

When I first began crafting stories, I pined for the title of "writer." What does it require, I mused, to be able to call oneself writer? A specific number of hours typing each week? A story appearing in a literary magazine? Or do you have to land a story in a publication that pays, or one that is as reputable as *Zyzzyva* or *Zoetrope*?

Within a few years, I understood that a writer is merely someone who writes, and once I acquired that identity for myself I never wanted to surrender it. I came to interpret life with a writerly mind, noting that this co-worker's dream about decapitating a pig must go into a story about dating and that Honolulu condo tower would be an ideal setting for a tale about a Japanese coquette. It was impossible for me to make a mistake in choosing a day job or lover because every moment of my suffering could become a paragraph in my oeuvre.

The problem with clutching to a writerly persona is that when your craft comes under criticism or you are unable to create your very being is threatened. You will have jeopardized your sense of self by constructing an imbalanced identity. The reality is that writing is only one of your daily functions, like sleeping or socializing or exercising. Yes, writers may differ from others due to their sensitivity or intuition, but if you locate your existence on a separate plane than "ordinary folk" then you are sealing yourself into a position of isolation and ignorance.

I recently viewed an Internet site claiming that one becomes a better writer by producing more words on a routine basis. The site set Stephen King as the masterly scribe, as he delivers about 10 pages—or 2,000 words each day. My advice to you is to occasionally break the schedule that allows you to call yourself writer. Go to a beach without a book or make word-less love to your partner during that time when you "should" be writing. For me, such a split in regimen is one of the most difficult things to do. Yet when I emerge from my writing cavern into the unfamiliar light of the world, my following work often gains a luminescence.

5. Be hollow

I frequently remind myself that the best part of my fiction writing doesn't come from me. Yes, I consciously shape the frame of a story, and select themes and name all characters. However, I don't actively implant moments of transcendence—those times when the story transports my reader to a point of thought loftier or more gorgeous than any word on the page. Where do these moments of transcendence come from, if not from my conscious self? My unconscious self? The web of consciousness strung above our heads and across the globe? Or perhaps spirits, or possibly what we call god?

I've decided I'm not meant to know but to trust. When we insert our ego into the work, it suffers. The story reveals the writer more than anything else, or it ceases to form completely due to that distracting relative of the ego we call inner critic.

If you aim to be hollow in your writing, and act as a kind of vessel, the fiction will always come. Maybe slowly, or even poorly at first. Yet if you keep your mind clear for something greater than yourself then I assure you something good will result. It may be universal truth through art or it may simply be pleasure from finishing what you began.

If you continually plug yourself with ego or cease trusting what words will arrive, you will most likely suffer from creative paralysis. Only after your ego withers from this condition and undergoes a necessary death will you start writing again.

6. Remember what a feat it is to create

When I abandoned writing, fiction seemed insignificant and writing a frivolous activity. What a waste of hours, I thought, all this dwelling on people who don't even exist and tweaking of imaginary situations. I could have spent those mid-week nights and weekend days career planning, or upgrading my apartment, or at least learning how to cook. Why be so impractical when I live in a society where the practical things like money and belongings and status matter above all else?

By quitting and returning to writing, I've acquired an answer to this question: I write in a practical world because this world won't last. When everything is impermanent—including one's existence—then what more miraculous activity is there than creating? Through our creations, we can understand this world before we exit it, and through our creations we can share that understanding with others.

I've noticed that an increase in age brings an increase in opposition to creativity. In the courses of their lifetimes, people lock themselves into all-consuming jobs, they assume responsibility for a spouse and/or child, they seal themselves inside an identity that can become a little more rigid with years or disappointments. I've met countless writers who've stopped writing. Their eyes light when they talk about that thriller they've outlined in their thoughts or the fictional biography that's been crystallizing in the back of the mind. But before they write, they require the perfect circumstance: when their sons leave for college, or when they locate that adequately lit cafe, or when they enroll in a writer's retreat to Arizona, or when they retire.

The truth is the perfect circumstance for writing is the one you're in right now. All writing requires is writing. The quality of the writing, the frequency of the writing, the results of the writing, and anybody's guidelines are all irrelevant. It is the act in itself that matters, and it is the act that can transform blank space into meaning, and a life that lacks into a life that is whole.

David Messengill gave his talk over a decade ago, and he continues to write fiction—and live in Seattle. He is the author of the novel *Red Swarm* (Montag Press) and the short story collection *Fragments of a Journal Salvaged from a Charred House in Germany, 1816* (Hammer and Anvil Books). His second novel is forthcoming from Montag Press. David's short works of literary and horror fiction have appeared in dozens of literary journals, including *Eclectica Magazine, Word Riot, The Raven Chronicles, Pulp Metal Magazine, Yellow Mama*, and *3 A.M. Magazine*, among others. Read free samples of his fiction at www.davidmassengill-fiction.com.

Holding Open the "Open of the World": On Pursuing the Craft of Poetry Just Now

Laura Gamache

September 14, 2006

...the artist's deepened concentration lets what may have previously been difficult to see enter the realm of the knowable and so be made available, both to artist and others.
—Jane Hirschfield, "Poetry and the Mind of Indirection," Nine Gates, p. 111

In the spring of 2005, a lump grew on the left side of my husband's neck. It grew fast. A few years before, I had had a lump in my breast that ballooned in a week. Fast growth was good, we learned then. It meant cyst. My husband's—Jim's—lump was cancer. We entered a country where neither of us spoke the language and both of us, our daughters too, were scared. We stumbled through terrain where sledgehammers came down on ants. We dwelt within the valley of the shadow of death.

Always collecting poetry books in other languages, mostly to use in teaching, I had one in a Scandinavian language, and no I don't want to know which. Transliterating the poems, trying to make sense in English, or sounds or both, that speak to what we went through.

Look up transliteration in the dictionary and you won't find a cipher for this form. There is an element of absurdity, of hopelessness, of the immense possibility of failure and futility, an omni-present not-understanding but trying to hear, a feeling of disconnect, at most partial-understanding, some surprised unearthings of what we actually went through that come through my dogged attempt to find them in the limited sounds of this language I do not speak as I did not speak the language of cancer or of doctors, all of us parlaying in a sort of incomplete unsatisfying patois. There were no reasons, just the experience. Jim is robustly well again, but nobody is spared.

Stephen Dunn writes:

Maybe one aspect of affirmation in poetry occurs when a poem offers language for our inarticulate understandings. It affirms what we vaguely already knew, makes us less strange to ourselves, invites us more fully into the human fold.
—*Stephen Dunn, Walking Light, p. 155*

I am trying to approach saying the unsayable about an experience that seems pandemic. So many friends and family have been through surgery, radiation, chemotherapy, the loss of what we thought was the solid ground of life only to find that the ground under all of us is shaking all the time. How do we live like this? With so much unsettling? Can I write it? Will it help? None of us gets that slip of paper that says, "For you 92 years, healthy, a quiet death in your sleep," or, "baby, live it up, sixteen more days, then poof." Life doesn't break promises. It doesn't make any.

Poetry, this made-thing I am so drawn to, does make promises, and, with craft and luck and concentration, a poem I make, you make, fulfills at least some of those promises. We know poems that have succeeded. We want to make those kinds of poems. Who will help? William Stafford says:

Yes

It could happen anytime, tornado
earthquake, Armageddon. It could happen.
Or sunshine, love, salvation.

It could you know. That's why we wake
and look out—no guarantees
in this life.

But some bonuses, like morning,
like right now, like noon,
like evening.
—William Stafford

I listen my way through the lines of my Scandinavian book, trying to find in its sounds a way to speak about last year. I have accumulated pages and pages of drafts for each poem I have worked through. The craft lies in going back and listening not only for our experience but for each remade poem's particular new music.

My first draft of poem 11 reads:

Yoda finds content:
Defends carlocks,
Defends gladwrap.

All any sound limbers are gardens and land
Foreswear them.

And here's another version:

Yaw that friends correct
debt fields collect
darts find gladness

all I need some little evidence that they'd
fuss over him.

Again, in Walking Light, Stephen Dunn says:

The revision process is when we worry the poem toward its virtues. We arrange and rearrange, suppress and add. We try to make it seem as if we danced all the way home.
—Stephen Dunn, Walking Light, p. 5

My current version of Poem 11 goes like this:

Imperatives

Jaded, find solace.
So debt fields collect,
defend gladness.

All I need, some little avenues, life
force, Jim.

As I work at this project, there are poems that cannot come through, much as I listen for and worry at them. Denise Levertov:

Hunting the Phoenix

Leaf through discolored manuscripts,
make sure no words
lie thirsting, bleeding,
waiting for rescue. No:
old loves half-
articulated, moments forced
out of the stream of perception
to play 'statue',
and never released
they had no blood to shed.
You must seek

the ashy nest itself
if you hope to find
charred feathers, smouldering flightbones,
and a twist of singing flame
rekindling.
—Denise Levertov

I am with her from the first line, leafing through folders, beginnings scrawled on the backs of teaching handouts, store receipts, the newspaper. And I too have had to say with her, "NO," though rarely do I throw them out.

That journal writing that forces moments out of the stream of perception to play "statue"—that careful description that still may have no life in it no matter how lovingly I have described the contents of the shelves at my grocery store, eight, nine, ten drafts still on my computer in the folder titled "Poetry No Hopers."

The poem tells me to do the work, to distrust an effortless composition process, to let go of poems with "no blood to shed." I nod in agreement, but then it opens its wings to bring me "smouldering flightbones" then "a twist of singing (or is it singe-ing) flame/rekindling" which is the hope that keeps me at this, and delectable language besides.

William Stafford mentors me through poetry and life:

Survival Course

This is the grip, like this:
both hands. You can close
your eyes if you like. When I say,
"Now," it's time. Don't wait
or it's all over. But not
too soon, either just right.

Don't worry. Let's go.
Both hands.
—William Stafford

Jane Hirschfield writes:

Image in particular, by gathering many energies toward a single end, creates an intense compression of meaning; it carries into the mind the solidity, particularity, and multifacetedness of actual objects. Such concreteness is a handle: it can be grasped. It must also be turned.
—Jane Hirschfield, Nine Gates, p. 114

We have all been shown the grip of the tennis racket, boat oar, reins, and this is a survival course, not middle-class recreation. Our lives, our poetry, are at stake. I started training as coxswain this summer, where I am learning about concise speech in real time. I cannot, as I do at my writing desk, close my eyes, because yes I often want to, the dark is fearsome but necessary, and pull my next word when it wants to come. In the boat, eight rowers depend on my words now. And now. I think this necessary not-bluster, this certainty of course can benefit my poetry. I may be wrong but we're going now. Stafford's poem says, "Now, it's time. Don't wait/or it's all over." This cuts me directly in the procrastination. It will all be over: the end of the world is personal for each of us.

And the end of our poetry—we struggle, and then we remember about the closed eyes and the two hands and the fact that time is finite, and we sit down to write, no matter how ill-equipped, pale-talented, dog-voiced. When we write, the writing makes us writers. There is satisfaction in that. I go to the shelf, read poets on poetry, read poems. I can be lost, as Mary Oliver has written, all day, for this is like picking blackberries. I go out with an empty pail, and in a few hours have filled both pail and stomach, my hands inky.

This morning, at Essential Baking on Madison, reading the Life & Arts section of the Seattle P.I., a gray shape the size of a football surged past my head into the paper. A water glass spilled, we woozed to our feet, a couple cowered by the door. A pigeon lifted its fat body on broad wings into the window, falling, flapping, and flattening itself into the glass. A barista carried a white baker's apron from the back, set it over the grounded bird, cradled it gently as a floured rising loaf, and walked it out the door. This might become a poem.

Jane Hirschfield says:

Frost described the poet's work as wandering through a field, allowing those burrs that will to stick to his pants an apt illustration of the meanderings of mind that are integral to the process of writing.
—Jane Hirschfield, Nine Gates, p. 120

Hirschfield adds:

Craft and consciousness matter. But a poet's attention must also be open to what is not already understood, decided, weighed out. For a poem to be fully alive, the poet needs to surrender the protection of the known and venture into a different relationship with the subject or is it object?
—Jane Hirschfield, Nine Gates, pp. 120-121

In the coffee shop of active confusion, what was my felt experience? The bird's?

The Polish poet, Zbigneiw Herbert, wrote in his poem:

I Would Like to Describe

I would like to describe the simplest emotion
joy or sadness

but not as others do
reaching for shafts of rain or sun

I would like to describe a light
which is being born in me
but I know it does not resemble
any star
for it is not so bright
not so pure
and it is uncertain

I would like to describe courage
without dragging behind me a dusty lion
and also anxiety
without shaking a glass of water

to put it another way
I would give all metaphors
in return for one word
drawn out of my breast like a rib
for one word
contained within the boundaries
of my skin
but apparently this is not possible

and just to say I love
I run around like mad
picking up handfuls of birds
and my tenderness
which after all is not made of water
asks the water for a face

and anger
different from fire

　　　　　　　　　The Writer's Craft

borrows from it
a loquacious tongue

so is blurred
so is blurred
in me
what whitehaired gentlemen
separated once and for all
and said
this is the subject
and this is the object

we fall asleep
with one hand under our head
and with the other in a mound of planets

our feet abandon us
and taste the earth
with their tiny roots
which next morning
we tear out painfully
—Zbigniew Herbert, trans. by Czeslaw Milosz and Peter Dale Scott

"we fall asleep/with one hand under our head/and with the other in a mound of planets"

Ah, a mound of planets.

"our feet abandon us/and taste the earth/with their tiny roots/which each morning/we tear out painfully"

Yes! We are beings of this earth, our bodies down to our feet know this, live it, even as our conscious, our logical, rational, linear minds want to pry us out of our animal selves, juggle stock market figures, flight schedules, deplore the wasting of time. We as poets want words, relationships with and between words, the spaces between them, to help us to taste the earth, to shock us awake into our lives again.

It amazes and puzzles me to be told I am a member of the "reality-based community." It is an incredible reversal to read that the neo-cons and President George W. are idealists.

Martin Heidegger, the philosopher, is helpful:

...since modern thinking is ever more resolutely and exclusively turning into calculation, it concentrates all available energy and 'interests' in calculating. This type of thinking is itself already the explosion of a power that could blast everything into nothingness.
—Martin Heidegger, On the Way to Language, p. 84.

Which makes me reflect on the words of a commentator on NPR today, who said of George W.'s Senior Advisor Karl Rove, and I paraphrase, that this guy is not some darkly evil lurker but a deeply pragmatic soul. Pragmatism may not be evil, but it does not go beyond or deeper than itself and is part of the power that could crush us, planet and all.

Heidegger says of the work we poets do:

To be a work means to set up a world. World is never an object that stands before us and can be seen. World is the ever-nonobjective to which we are subject as long as the paths of birth and death, blessing and curse keep us transported into Being. The work as work sets up a world. The work holds open the Open of the world.
—Martin Heidegger, Poetry, Language, Thought, pp. 44-45.

Pragmatists and cynics cannot hold open the Open of the world. That is the poet's work. And our work is needed. Poet and teaching artist Laura Gamache earned an MFA in Creative Writing at the University of

Washington, where she directed the Writers in the Schools MFA Internship Program for 10 years. She has published two chapbooks: "Never Enough" in 2017 and "Nothing to Hold Onto" in 2005. Her poems and teaching essays have appeared in many print and on-line journals and anthologies, including WA129 in 2017. She has had the privilege of writing and reading with students as a WITS writer since 1997.

Susan Rich

Poems, Pastries, and Politics

Nov. 9, 2006

Why connect the writing of poetry with an appreciation of good food?

On first consideration, the juxtaposition of poems and pastries might seem frivolous. Isn't poetry sustenance for something more than the physical body?

Recently, I taught a workshop at a local college advertised as "O Taste and Write: Food Poems" and perhaps a subtext of free food is why sixty people appeared on a Tuesday afternoon ready to create poems. And why not? Isn't a poem that takes your head off and a sumptuous *crème brûlée* both causes for celebration? Doesn't each experience awaken its audience with a sensory jolt, tossing us deeper into the world?

When pomegranate crisps and madeleines first appeared in my work, I was somewhat embarrassed. My years as a staff person with Oxfam America, and then Amnesty International, imbued me with a core belief in humanity from a critical perspective. How could I move from poems about international human rights abuses to poems inspired by the cereal aisle?

Let me explain. After my first book, *The Cartographer's Tongue, Poems of the World* appeared, focusing on my experiences in Africa and the Middle East, it seemed reasonable that I'd keep exploring human rights issues. I tried, as best I could, to call attention to the women and men I had met who lived more courageous and complex lives than my own.

I wrote about Yves-Rose, on her sixteenth birthday, how she found her father's mutilated body on the family's front porch steps—a gift from the Ton-Ton Macoute. I wrote about Giovanni Soto, a Guatemalan street kid, disappeared by the Guatemalan police, and poems of middle-aged Bosnian Muslims bombed by their neighbors as they hid under the stairs in a spot meant for preserving potatoes, not people. In short, I believed in poetry of witness. Poems, to my mind, needed to change the world.

And while I still believe that and I still write poems concerning the civil war in Somalia and the ongoing war in Iraq, I also believe deeply in interweaving these poems with ones that focus on the direct dailiness of bread and wine. Food poems allow me to look at my subject sideways, to explore baked goods as a metaphor for grief or the grocery store as a stand-in for childhood. I don't worry about whether I am misrepresenting a sun gold tomato or positioning a tiramisu in an unfavorable light. And a mix of watermelon seeds and war crimes may be where my imaginative strength lives.

If poetry can change the world, someone has to read it, someone has to be moved to care about a mother dodging bullets in Mogadishu, a young boy shot by Israeli forces in the political quagmire of Gaza City. I don't want to conjure a world of despair but rather a world as vibrant and alive as any I have ever experienced. The comfort of a family supper or the Dreamsicles of a corner grocer might, in the end, prove more vital to the story than the type of explosives used or which political party abused its power.

I'd like to share some ways that I've folded food imagery into my poems. Perhaps these suggestions might inspire others to create new work. Poems, pastries, and politics might someday cook-up an utterly different kind of cuisine, one that ameliorates the human spirit as well as the body.

Write a food poem of exaggeration.

This is an opportunity to play. Write a poem exaggerating your appreciation or distaste for a food you know well. Permit yourself to go wild. I began a recent workshop asking participants to introduce themselves by naming a food they loved or hated. "I'm Stan and I loathe lobster" one older man proclaimed, "I'm in love with a wild salmon," a nursing student confessed. "A cheddar sharper than I am ought be outlawed," another participant demanded. The results included a poem where a salmon stood in for an erotic lover and an aged cheddar cheese began a meditation for one woman's self-reflection.

Try a historical appreciation of the eggplant or an ode to an artichoke.

This poem requires research. How fun to delve into the history of what we eat. For a poem still in progress I've learned the lurid past of the eggplant and why the Imam fainted, as in the fabled Middle Eastern eggplant dish. While researching a poem concerning the fantasies of a lonely baker, I found one website, www.epicurious.com, that listed over eight hundred different kinds of cake. Intersperse historical fact with your own taste sensations to create thirteen ways of looking at an artichoke.

Challenge yourself to write a political poem that uses food as a central image.

There was a common joke among Palestinians in the early 1990's before the creation of the Palestinian Authority that referred to the fact that the red, green and black colors of the Palestinian flag had been outlawed by the Israeli government. "Did you hear," the joke went, the Israelis have outlawed watermelons! It's a common site to see farmers selling watermelons in late summer by the side of the road. In Gaza, watermelons were political. Write a poem where a food is inextricably linked with a social cause.

In "First Supper at Salama's" [Rich, Susan *Bellingham Review*, Volume XXIX, No. 2, Issue #58] a Somali man offers his country's specially prepared bread and meat along with political commentary.

Ghazal for the Woman from Vitez

It's the best watermelon in the world
but there's no way to say it in words.

She had squatted in the space for apples and pears
under the staircase, a year, beyond the place of words.

Now she comes back with tea, examines me closely,
my out-of-date phrase book, my mispronounced words.

I ask for the toilet and she shows me the bedrooms, bombed
by neighbors who should have known how to use words.

We walk out to her garden in late afternoon light,
survey squash plants and corn stalks, we re-enter words.

In Bosnian the tomato is called paradise, sweetness
transferred from some other country's words.

We drink rounds of whisky, call her sons on the phone
laughing because we have found our way out through words.

Reprinted from Susan Rich, *The Cartographer's Tongue: Poems of the World*, White Pine Press, NY

Susan Rich is the author of four collections of poems: *Cloud Pharmacy The Alchemist's Kitchen, Cures Include Travel,* and *The Cartographer's Tongue: Poems of the World which won the PEN USA Award for Poetry and the Peace Corps Writers Award.* She co-edited an anthology of essays from the Poetry Foundation: *The Strangest of Theatres: Poets Crossing Borders.* Rich's poems have appeared in the *Alaska Quarterly Review, Harvard Review, World Literature Today* and elsewhere. *She is a co-curator of Words West Literary and co-founder of Poets On the Coast: A Writing Retreat for Women. You can visit her on the web at www.susanrich.net.*

Memory, Mapping and Imagination

Kay Mullen

April 12, 2007

I want to share briefly some thoughts about Memory, Mapping and Imagination as they relate to my book, *A Long Remembering: Return to Vietnam*: why and how the poems came to be written. While this is a craft talk and not a reading, I will include several short poems as examples of points I want to make about this topic.

My book contains poems around the experience of returning to Vietnam in 2000 with 15 young adoptees and their parents twenty five years after the end of the war in 1975 These young people were returning for the first time to their homeland. Most were infants or toddlers when they left Vietnam. This was a first trip for parents. I was among this group of 35, as was my husband, AJ, and our 26 year old son, Timothy. It was this trip that gave these young adoptees the memories they needed to discover who they were, where they came from, what the future might hold for them.   It was the task of this journey back to Vietnam to restore some of those lost memories, to support these young people in their search for identity.

I realized the significance of memory as we traveled. I wanted to know what poets had to say about it. Because of time constraints I will mention only two. Jane Hirshfield, in her book, Nine Gates, speaks of poetry as a "Vessel of Remembrance." She says that without the power of memory, creativity as it flows without end from the source of our being, there would be nothing to connect one moment to the next. Poetry is language put into forms of remembrance. Without memory, the world would have no way to carry forward all that has gone before." Hirshfield goes on to say, "We peer into the new poem with the old hope:

that we might find there a few words to illumine more widely our passage through the dark woods and brightly lit cities of this fleeting, time-bound world. And the art of poetry remains a daughter of Remembrance of our wish to feel joined to some fabric that both gives meaning to and is made meaningful by the part of it we are." (p. 177)

Another poet, Peter Davison, says in his forward to Breathing Room, "to remember is to keep things that have already happened from siding into oblivion." Had these young people not returned to Vietnam, the memories might well have "slid into oblivion." They may never have known the stories of those early months and years of their lives, nor the people and places that helped form who they were. By returning to their orphanages and talking with those who remembered them, by understanding more fully their people, their land and culture, the memories were restored and new ones were created throughout the trip.

This book, *A Long Remembering: Return to Vietnam*, is very much a vessel of remembrance. In writing these poems I hoped to create memories for our adopted son, but also for the other young adoptees and their parents. Even though each person in that group created memories of their own, poems held in memory can sustain us when times are difficult and also offer the discovery of poetry's power. Memories connect us to one another. We have all known that sense of belonging and acceptance when others have listened to our experiences.

These young adults were searching for meaning in their lives. They were searching for their identity. They grieved, and although their grief had been suppressed, it was a loss they carried through the years. Although they were adopted into loving families, they grieved for the loss of their homeland, their people, their culture and history. It was important to restore these memories and to reconnect moments of the past, to piece together the past so that the future could once again have meaning. An example of how this grief had been suppressed and began to surface shortly after we arrived, can be seen in this poem. (p. 13)

First Meal in Vietnam

On the day of arrival, we gather for our first meal
in Ho Chi Minh city: ginger rice, shrimp cakes
and bean sprouts, sesame asparagus, a treat
of sweet dragon fruit. Without warning, one
young man bends his shoulders, bursts into sobs
as if some long buried ache suddenly awakened
to pain. Who are his parents, why did they leave
him, how can he thread his life, stitch his future
with strong ties and peace? For a moment he
seems separated from the people in the room.
He knows he is free to express his fears at what
he may find, what he has lost. Tears fall
from many faces. Twenty-five years of unknowns
begin to unravel here at this long table. He
cannot yet put into words what he wants to say.
Some words may never be spoken.

In one of his lectures at PLU, Kent Meyers said, "We may need to break our memories down into manageable, connected segments that allow us to concentrate and distill them in a meaningful way." This was my task as I returned from Vietnam. It was at least two years after the trip ended that I began to write the poems using a few notes I had taken and the itinerary listing each day's events. My memory served me well. Details came back to me with seemingly little effort mainly I believe because these were once-in-a lifetime experiences, very vivid and memorable. I began to break down the memories into segments as Meyers suggested and think about ways to map the experiences. I also did a good deal of research around these poems. Mapping a poem, as I understand it, means to look at the poem's geography or landscape … to look at the physical, emotional, aesthetic, intellectual and linguistic aspects of a poem. Mapping includes words, word associations, phrases, facts, objects, ideas and so on.

One example of Mapping a poem came from a visit to a lacquer factory: the circumstances, remembering words and phrases to recreate the event, what it meant in terms of the men working there, of the facets that made up the process. So I came up with words that grounded the poem in terms of place and facts, in terms of time and materials and in terms of a certain meaning invested in the young men there and what it meant in metaphorical terms.

I like to think of mapping a poem a little like breaking bread, of naming and gathering the ingredients and putting them together to create something new. As with the baking of bread, I had to mix and knead the poem's ingredients, let the poem, like dough sit a while, and return to it, until, like bread, it is ready to be placed in the oven, and like a poem, in the heat of the imagination so that eventually I would have that loaf, that poem I was creating. What happens in the oven baking bread is as mysterious as what happens when a poem is being created. No one can explain transformation; how dough becomes bread nor how the imagination creates a poem. It is the great mystery of baking and of the power of poetry.

I'll read a poem about an experience in Vietnam. I researched and mapped the essentials of the experience. (p. 24)

The Lacquer Factory

In Hue, twelve young men sit
at long tables against a wall.
They neither look up nor smile,
intent on laborious lacquer
techniques. Their hands
blackened with rosin,
apply as many as twelve times
to sanded and polished wood.
It is the mother-of-pearl inlay,

the gold dust and eggshell
that yields the final shine.

The work goes on where fans
spread heat and fumes.
Men paint and brush, cut
and seal when the inset
is primed. A gleam of oil
on their hands reflects the onyx
                    displays on the lacquer-ware
shelves. Their sweaty faces
mirror the gloss of every piece.

These young men took great pride in the difficult work they were doing. They seemed to have created for themselves both an inner and outer accomplishment as they bent to the work they knew would bring satisfaction to themselves and to many others.

The following poem comes out of my imagination. Because our son had no knowledge of his parents, I wanted to create imaginary parents so that he would have a sense of how much he was loved, how they wanted him safe at all costs. He grew up with this awareness. So with the understanding I had about Vietnamese men and women, about the war and circumstances at the end of it, I created an imaginary father and mother. This is the poem about his Vietnamese father. (p. 34)

A Father's Legacy

> *At twenty-six he falls*
> *on the leaf-soaked jungle,*
> *dies inching along on his belly.*

He takes a scrap of paper
from his jacket. A sliver of light

through the forest is all he needs.
He pulls the wedding picture from
his pocket, a thumb-print
of blood on a note to his child;

> *If I don't return, if I'm not there*
> *to see you*

for the first time,
when you speak first words,
when you grow
to be the best you can,
I'll be in your dreams,
in your words, your flesh.
My child,
don't grieve for me,
believe in yourself.
Have nothing to do
with war.

In conclusion, as Hirshfield says, poetry is a vessel of remembrance. *Memories* give us a sense of identity. They offer healing and insights. They connect us to the past and to one another so we can move with greater confidence into the future. *Mapping* poems gets the poet in touch with the poem's essentials: to know the geography of the poem, where it is leading, where it might take us. The task of the *Imagination* is to transform in some mysterious way, to be in touch with the creative energy and power of a poem.

I'd like to end with a quote from the poet, Muriel Rukeyser: "I don't believe that poetry can save the world. I do believe that the forces in us wish to share something of our experience by turning it into something and giving it to somebody: that is poetry. That is some kind of saving thing, and as far as my life is concerned, poetry has saved me again and again." Perhaps these poems will offer some "saving thing" for the young adult adoptees who traveled so far to gain a greater understanding of themselves and perhaps for the parents and those who read or hear the poems.

Bibliography

Davison, Peter. "Catches of Breath: A Foreword," in *Breathing Room*, New York: Knopf, 2000, p. ix..
Hirshfield, Jane. *Nine Gates: Entering the Mind of Poetry*. New York: Harper,
1998. pp. 177, 196
Meyers, Kent. *Lecture*, Pacific Lutheran University, August 2006.
Rukeyser, Muriel, Clement Greenberg, Translator. *Community Archive*, Vol. 19, No. 3, March 1955.

Kay Mullen's work has appeared in *Valparaiso Poetry Review, Floating Bridge Review, Appalachia, San Pedro River Review, American Life in Poetry* and others, as well as Anthologies including *Pontoon* and *Becoming: What Makes a Woman*. She has authored three full-length poetry collections, her latest, *Even the Stones*, in memory of her deceased husband. Her honors include the Washington State William Stafford award, Best of the Net and Pushcart prize nominations. Kay received her MFA Rainier Writing Workshop from Pacific Lutheran University. She lives and teaches in Tacoma.
Presented at the It's About Time Writers Reading Series, Seattle, WA., Thursday, October 14, 2004

Master Guides on the Revision Trail

John McFarland

(from First Steps and First Words Onward)

Tonight I brought along a cartoon strip that shows and tells about a classic situation we all find ourselves in from time to time. Here we meet a hard-working writer who has had an inspiration and written it down in a late-night frenzy. In the morning he pulls what he has written from the typewriter (this is an old cartoon strip), reads it and says, "I thought this was good when I wrote it last night! It stinks!"

We know the sinking feeling of this fellow writer, unfortunately we know it well. But there is good news: (1) the writer in the cartoon strip has spotted a problem with his latest work early; and (2) he may be able to fix it. It is not too late. And this is where craft comes into play, along with courage and faith. Never forget those either.

We generally can agree on what courage and faith are, but what specifically do we mean by the term "craft"? There seem to be as many definitions of craft as there are writers-every month Esther invites a new one of us to report on our angle.

One of my primary resources as a writer is the dictionary, and so let me tell you some of what I found there. The dictionary's definitions of craft talk about: (1) the artful construction of a text or discourse, well-wrought writing, and (2) skill in doing or making something. Proficiency. These definitions certainly provide a starting point for thinking about craft, but, for each of us, the words artful, well-wrought and proficient may take on very different meanings depending on our goals or our audiences.

Rather than confusing the issue by going down too many paths at once, I'll focus on the challenges the writer of short fiction faces: stories are by definition short; they must be artfully focused but somehow rich at the same time. Their brevity, the experts say, puts extra pressure on the very beginning of a story: in the finished story the start may have to be a literal taking-off point. Yet, what you write for the beginning in an early draft may be just something/anything to start; and all too often, if you read over that early draft beginning too soon, you find yourself in the same shoes as our friend in the third panel of the cartoon strip: what you wrote down first may really, really stink. Others may tell you to revise the beginning until you're happier with it. My advice is: don't worry about it too early. Bad first lines happen to the best of writers; some truly great writers, in fact, publish finished stories with openings that strain a reader's patience, even a fan's patience.

Here's one example from Henry James:

"I had simply, I supposed, a change of heart, and it must have begun when I received my manuscript from Mr. Pinhorn." (from "The Death of the Lion")

Now, those of us who read James and love his work know that the rest of the story may have a payoff that is not evident in this less-than-thrilling opening line, and we may allow him a little longer to get going. But what if we were browsing through a collection of a writer we didn't know at all, say a collection by the Nobel-laureate German writer Heinrich Böl, and we happened to open the book to a story which starts with the line: "While I was standing on the dock watching the seagulls, my sad face attracted the attention of a policeman on his rounds." (from "My Sad Face")?

Even if we regard these opening lines from Henry James and Heinrich Böl as serviceable, in the sense that they are setting the scene or tone (as William Trevor does with the pedestrian line, "The rectory was in County Wexford, eight miles from Ennisworthy." [from "Autumn Sunshine"]), there is no way that we will say after reading the whole story that the opening line was the most memorable one in the story and there is no rule that says it has to be. OK, let's assume that we accept the opening line as serviceable; but we also have to be honest with ourselves: when we read such lines we are waiting for something to start and we are already slightly bored. And if we are bored and ready to stop reading the work of the famous and acclaimed, we know in our bones what mystery writer Jane Langton refers to when she advises, "You've got to be aware that the reader is probably reading in a hurry . . . (and) you cannot be boring." (from "A Literary Life: Talking with Jane Langton," by Susan Lumenello, Harvard University GSAS Colloquy, Summer 2003, pp. 10-11).

What's more, once we've read the Paris Review Interviews with Authors series, we also won't be able to push aside Tennessee Williams's opinion that if you feel you're losing an audience's attention, you have to do something, anything, to get it back even if you have to shoot someone onstage. Our own instincts as readers and the wise words offered by our guides, the more seasoned writers, tell us one thing: building the potential for boredom into an opening is something to be avoided.

Though we don't want to back ourselves into a corner where we feel compelled to be melodramatic or merely "entertaining," there are many alternatives to taking the risk James, Böll and Trevor dared in these stories I've mentioned. Here are a few:
(1) "In Paris there are certain streets which are in as much disrepute as any man branded with infamy can be." Honoré de Balzac (trans. Herbert J. Hunt), from "Ferragus: Chief of the Companions of Duty"
or, (2) "Miss Diana never used the peep hole in her front door." Pedro Zarraluki (trans. Jason Wilson), from "The Gallant Ghost"
or, (3) "'Ooh! This is Hell! We're entering the jaws of Hell!' shrieked Marga." Ana Maria Moix (trans. Dinny Thorold), from "That Red-Headed Boy I See Every Day"

These first lines prompt me as a reader to cry out, "And? . . . And?" Reading them, I am most definitely not bored and I really want to know what comes next.

In these particular first lines we find: (1) sheer beauty of language or a vitality that hooks us (as in the Balzac), (2) mystery that draws us in (as in Zarraluki), or (3) a line that telegraphs what will come, but in a sly, enticing way, not by giving away the whole show right off the bat. When a first line is effective in holding our attention and keeping it, we feel less bored and more secure that the next lines the writer will unfold for us will build on that. For a short story writer, this is the best insurance we can buy.

In my own work, I show a distinct bias toward the third approach: the hint that telegraphs. For example, a few of my first lines are:

"Most days Momma bent over backwards to be a walking example." (from "No Fault")
"Others could laugh, but David was a believer." (from "Evenings Out")
"Joel Winwood's bright red shirt with its green piping made him look like a pincushion." (from "Jimmy's Class")

I feel that if my first line intrigues the reader, then I've earned some breathing space to develop my story. But I'm here to report that in none of these cases was the first line that appears in the final, published version of the story in the first draft, not in the first line or anywhere else. And what I've found is that the line that eventually takes its place at the beginning of a story actually grows out of the story as the story is reworked and reworked and reworked. For me in the process of revising, the story evolves and seems to grow its own beginning. That's my good news; but there's bad news too. Revisions seem to proceed uniquely for each story: there is no formula, there is no set number of revisions. My only guideline is that I'll know when it's done, if I live through it. (It's the rare writer who can join Anita Brookner, the brilliant author of *Hotel du Lac* and other novels, in saying that she only writes one draft of her books. Her first draft is the final version, no revisions, no fortieth draft, she sits down, writes it out and she's done. For the rest of us, though . . . well, we can only envy her.)

Practice and reading other people's work has honed my instincts for knowing when the story is done and doing that has also developed my ability to see when it works and when it doesn't. And I always keep in mind what Mark Twain said: "The difference between the right word and the almost right word is like the difference between lightning and a lightning bug."

That genuine jolt Twain is talking about is one example of the thrill factor that I feel we must always strive to build into our stories. In his novel Finnie Walsh, Steven Galloway is in the midst of describing a familiar hockey maneuver that Finnie is executing on the ice when Finnie adds something spicy and unique to the old move, surprising his audience where they weren't expecting it; Galloway then comments: "this only served to increase Finnie's popularity with both sexes; nothing was as attractive as skill and unpredictability." (pp. 91-92) And so here Galloway is talking about the thrill factor in the hockey move (which he captured), but he's also captured the essence of how he did it as a writer: skill and unpredictability; the hint and the invitation. We all have to master doing both together, with perfect timing and precision, or else we won't carry it off; and if it fails, we look pretentious, clumsy or too far-out. The right words in the right combination at the right time give you Twain's lightning. Let's talk about some ways of making lightning strike on a regular basis.

A few years ago I was working with the editor of an anthology and he suggested one small change to the story I'd sent him. It was a simple change and it involved the very first word a reader would see: the title. I had called my story "Playtime." What the editor suggested was to add an exclamation mark to transform my title into "Playtime!" It's simple, yes, but it was also colossal: all of a sudden the story announced itself with authority; from its title alone you know that things will get rolling fast and that you should probably expect a good time. The exclamation mark brought that extra oomph that made the story that much more itself, like the twist of lemon in your cocktail, or the accessory that makes an ensemble work together, the expert flair. To me, this was the best kind of editorial prodding and collaboration, and that experience has helped sharpen my own editorial eye.

Another example illustrates this principle in another way: I recently won a contest with a new story. When I started working on this story it carried the title "Airing." I thought at the time that it was going to be about Opening Up and Letting In the Air. Only after many revisions did I see the story had to begin with the narrator stating that he was very sure of his attitude toward current arrangements in his life. In the first line, he says, "I didn't need a boyfriend. I already had one and he was a keeper." As the story evolved, however, it became clear that although he may not have needed another boyfriend, he finds other things he and many people like him do need: friendship, brotherhood, respect, trust and equal protection under the law. That arc of the narrator's growth, going from the certainty of Not Needing one narrowly defined thing to an awareness of a broader sense of Needing, was a surprise to me, and so I changed the title to "Not Needing, Needing." That title, which grew organically out of the story, may not make complete sense to a reader until after reading the story, yet I felt it was the perfect title for it, and perhaps the only one. Once I had that title, and the first line set the stage with authority, solutions to many of the nagging questions I had about the body of the story came into focus and the entire piece fell quickly into place for me. Not only that, after the fact, I discovered that the term, "Not Needing, Needing," is a concept in the work of the psychoanalyst Abraham Maslow (famous for his work on "peak experience" and "self-actualization"). I had never heard of that concept before, but it fits in miraculously well with what turned out to be the theme of the finished story.

Up to now, I have been talking about ideal situations and words of wisdom from our chosen guides, but I have also brought a real-life example with me. A while back, I wrote a draft of a story that I called "Simple Happiness." Its first two paragraphs are:

The Writer's Craft

Simple Happiness

Paula had decided it was easier to go than to stay away. Staring Nathan down, she asked, "What should I bring?"

"You're actually coming?" The exhausted monotone of what he called "Mr. Nathan's afternoon voice" perked up in astonishment that Paula was saying yes to the standing invitation to his Friday get-togethers.

Later on in the story the tension set up in these first two paragraphs changes in surprising ways and really the "simple" of the title isn't so simple; as I re-read the opening in this draft, I felt it was OK, but I also felt it was stalling. It was perhaps asking the reader to cut Nathan and Paula too much slack, to let them, still complete strangers to the reader, meander when really the reader may want them to get off the dime. But what ultimately motivated me to change what seemed perfectly service-able was that I eliminated parts of a later scene, in that one, Paula has a hangover when she confronts the concept of simple happiness and acknowledges how hard it is for her to accept that it can actually exist. Once the section of that scene with its reference to "simple happiness" was gone, the title made absolutely no sense. Without that, though, the real thrust of the story emerged more clearly for me, and I could speed it along. I found then that that section of the scene and the title it brought up were actually obstacles to my making the story a tight whole. And so I changed the title, and loosened up the beginning in a way that lets the reader inside Paula's emotions faster and less ambiguously. And here is the beginning as I changed it:

Saviors

Paula was in a bind. Nathan had just invited her to another of his regular Friday get-togethers and seemed about to crash and burn in front of her eyes. She really didn't want to go, but in the end this time it was easier to accept than to cook up an excuse to stay away. "What should I bring?" she asked.

The effect was miraculous. Nathan bounced back from the edge. "You'll actually come? Jimmy will die!"

These changes may seem minor or inconsequential as I read them to you here, but in the context of the whole story, I feel they are critical the beginning of the "Saviors" version works better in setting up the tensions that will be extended and upended in the course of the story. And, what's more, and this is the most important thing, when I read the opening to "Saviors" I don't have the sinking feeling our friend exhibits in the cartoon strip: I have taken what made me cringe in the early draft of "Simple Happiness" and saved it from itself.

My first published writing was film criticism and book reviews, essentially journalism. There, the requirements are spelled out by your editor and the standards set by those who have preceded you, a very different situation from the anything-goes rules of writing poetry or fiction. But I learned important lessons as a creative writer from journalism: conciseness, awareness of your audience and its expectations, and, most of all, what sets you apart is how you introduce the thrill factor into your work. Never forget personality, and never underestimate its power.

And let me end with one last quote, this one from Guy Davenport, another writer worth checking out, writing in The New York Times Book Review in 1982: "Two people attentive to a detail of the world make a society, and the object they find significant has crossed over from meaninglessness to symbol. Art is always the replacing of indifference by attention."

Once again, the wise words offered by our guides, the more seasoned writers, tell us that the work of attention to detail, and transforming that detail from meaninglessness to universal meaning or symbol, is, ultimately, our craft, our magic and our goal.

First Presented at the "It's About Time Reading Series," Edition #183, on October 14, 2004, as one author's perspective on The Writer's Craft

John McFarland is a short story writer, essayist and critic. His fiction and essays have appeared in the literary journals Ararat, Caliban and StringTown as well as in the anthologies The Next Parish Over: A Collection of Irish-American Writing (New Rivers Press, 1993) and The Isherwood Century: Essays on the Life and Work of Christopher Isherwood (University of Wisconsin Press, 2000). His book for young readers, The Exploding Frog: and Other Fables from Aesop (Little Brown, 1981) was selected by Parents Choice Magazine as one of the best illustrated-books of 1981. His story "A Secret of the Andes" won First Prize, Children's Picture Book Category, at the 1992 Pacific Northwest Writers Conference and was later published as a centerpiece in Cricket Magazine's soccer issue of September 1997. Most recently, his short story "Not Needing, Needing" was selected as the winner of Frontiers Newsmagazine's first short fiction contest. He lives in Seattle, Washington.

The Independent Candidate, or how to have an accomplished writer's life without an MFA

Tamara Sellman

February 8, 2007

Many of today's undiscovered writers feel a tremendous pressure to earn an MFA (Master of Fine Arts) in Creative Writing in order to give legitimacy to their writing careers.

I'm here to discuss the possibility that this is a manufactured notion about the contemporary writing life. In fact, you do not need an MFA to succeed. Period.

I used to struggle with the possibility of attending grad school to the point that, in 1994, I actually registered for the MFA at Columbia in Chicago. A couple of weeks later, I bowed out after learning I was pregnant. I realized the 3-hour round-trip commute, the added homework and the schedule were not things I could integrate into my new life as a mother.

After that, I continued to reconsider the possibility, but found myself saying No every time mostly because I didn't have the money or the time.

The first few times I said No, I felt envious of those who did have the money and time. Sound familiar?

Then I rebelled against the whole notion after my writing took a left-hand turn and was no longer traditional or particularly welcome in the grad school environment at that time.

It was in my late 30s that I realized I was doing, to a certain degree (no pun intended), the things I thought I would only be able to do with an MFA.

This will not be an impeachment of MFA programs. If I had the time and the money, I would enter a program. I love school. I love the collegiate landscape, the homework, the learning. I'm a nerd. So, maybe when I'm retired... But for now, like many of you, I simply can't.

Instead, I'm here to question the notion that MFAs are the only path to successful creative writing careers. I will debunk myths about writing programs, provide you with evidence that writers can succeed without advanced degrees and then offer you tactics for replicating the MFA experience for yourself.

I. On matters of higher learning

True or False: An MFA offers writers the chance to work with professionals to learn what they couldn't otherwise.

True: But there are workshop facilitators, continuing education instructors, coaches and mentors also available for this very thing. Writers conferences, open to all, feature the considerable teaching talents of successful authors. We can even learn from cohorts in our own writing groups.

There's always something to learn. Grad school isn't the only place to learn it.

True or False: An MFA program allows people to carve out two to three years to focus on writing.

True: But any serious writer can do this without an MFA by making a plan and sticking to it. It's all about time management and setting priorities. Of all the people who write novels during National Novel Writing Month, how many have MFAs? I've achieved this goal 3 times, and I don't have an MFA.

True or False: The MFA is the only way you'll be able to keep your butt in the chair for many hours a day and not answer the phone or your e-mail.

False: All serious writers do this, regardless their homework, their workload or their family obligations. Don't you?

Evidence: Burn this into your skulls: The late Andre Dubus II once admitted that he would have eventually mastered what he'd learned through the Iowa Writers' Workshop all on his own.

II. On matters of structure

True or False: An MFA is a shortcut that helps instill discipline.

False: MFA programs do not exist to teach you discipline. They exist to help you become a better writer than you were going in. They also exist to train future creative writing teachers. That's about it.

Plenty of MFA grads give up within a year of receiving their degrees because they can't deal with the patience and persistence that the writing life requires.

What is discipline but the lassoing of patience and persistence? I can't stress it enough. You can only learn discipline through your own efforts.

True or False: It's harder to be a writer without an MFA.

False: If you know anyone in an MFA, you know how exhausted they are. Let's face it: writing is hard work for everyone. Period.

True or False: It will take longer to have a writing career if you don't have an MFA.

False: There is no average career-development period for any writer. This isn't a footrace, folks, nor is the MFA a charmed pit stop. Writing comes when it comes, training or no training.

Evidence: Author Daniel Handler, a.k.a. Lemony Snicket, graduated with an undergraduate degree, got a "brainless part-time job that paid just enough to live on" and started writing.

In a recent interview, Handler said, "I couldn't imagine what else to do. I had no other plans. I thought, 'If I'm going to waste these years, at least I'll have a huge stack of papers to show for it.' "

He spent the first year and a half of his post-university life writing a novel he eventually threw away. Handler quite accurately suggests that "You need the time to learn, and the time to screw up and the time to write a book and throw it away. That takes a while. If you can get that without an MFA, fine." Handler, in fact, did.

III. On matters of talent, ambition and excellence

True or False: First-time novelists without MFAs and few credits are only capable of writing thinly-veiled autobiography.

False: The careers of Stephen King, Mitch Albom and Daniel Handler don't fit this assumption; neither does yours, I'm sure.

True or False: The MFA guarantees you'll be a better writer.

False: I'm an editor. After having read thousands of manuscript submissions from both MFAs and non-MFAs, I have not seen a compelling difference in the quality of one group of writings over another. Countless other editors will echo this finding.

True or False: You get a better education in critical reading and thinking with an MFA.

False: An MFA offers an established educational menu, but you, as a writer, can also set this up for yourself. If you can read and think, you can improve your critical and analytical abilities just as well without an MFA. It requires that you have the wealth of curiosity and discipline to direct your own education.

Writers without MFAs can still do this by exposing themselves to other great writers and to great literature. The venues are there: libraries, writing workshops, continuing education programs, book discussion groups, the Internet. The sky's the limit.

Evidence: Writers who have succeeded independently of the grad school ivory tower include Mary Oliver, William Carlos Williams, Lucille Clifton, John Steinbeck, Carson McCullers, Ray Bradbury, Anne Sexton, Louis L'Amour, Susan Sontag, Walter Mosley, Betty Friedan, Stephen King and many many others.

More evidence: Independent thinking's day is coming has come. This has relevance to the world of creative writing. Stay with me for a minute.

According to new studies done by the think tank organization Demos, independent scholarship, what they call the Pro-Am revolution, may become the way we define intellectualism in the 21st century.

"For Pro-Ams, leisure is not passive consumerism but active and participatory, it involves the deployment of publicly accredited knowledge and skills, often built up over a long career, which has involved sacrifices and frustrations."

Further: William Ivins Jr. was not a writer, but he was the accomplished curator at New York's Metropolitan Museum of Art for 30 years where he amassed one of the world's largest encyclopedic repositories of printed images.

Unlike his contemporaries, he held no advanced degrees. He was self-taught in art history and worked in other unrelated trades like law and stock brokering.

However, his personal interest in art compelled him to review tens of thousands of prints over his early adult life. It was this intimate self-education that led him to become one of the world's most respected curators.

Ivins' example demonstrates that part of this journey we're on requires that we take our interests to heart, that we invest our time in pursuits that aren't always practical, and that we apply our passion to our work. This, not an advanced degree, is more likely to lead us to success in our creative lives.

With these things in mind, I'd like to close by offering a baker's dozen tactics you can take to replicate the MFA experience for yourself.

1. Make time: commit yourself to a schedule made on your own terms. Use that time to cleave away at the sculpture of your stories, poems, narratives and novels. Do not do the dishes. Do not answer the phone. Writing time is writing time.

2. Adopt a structure for learning: Build in learning time. Make a weekly date at the library or online. Read related work during your lunch break. Turn personal vacations into fact-finding missions, when you can. Be a student of life.

3. Find a mentor: Hook up with someone willing and able to help who has progressed further in their writing career. They don't have to be

university affiliates. They can even be friends who are artists, writers or teachers, as long as they're there to help you move toward your goals.

4. Seek motivation: Join writing groups to keep your finger in the pie. Write blogs about your writing life to keep yourself on task. Go to live readings and revel in the pleasures of inspiration.

5. Find community: Organized writing communities abound both in "Real Life" and online. Tap into all that interest you, but make sure you still prioritize your time for writing first. Writing is still a solitary activity; communities are for support and do not replace the real work ahead.

6. Read: Everything. Everyday.

7. Write: Just do it. Ten words one day, a thousand the next … it's ALL writing.

8. Draft an honest mission statement: Like resolutions, these have a way of sticking once you put them to paper. Assign yourself a plan that includes, in concrete detail, what you'll do, how long it will take and what you hope to accomplish. Hold yourself to it to the very end.

9. Aspire to be a connoisseur: They don't say Write What You Know for nothing. Find those 2 or 3 topics that excite you and make them your focus during the period of your mission statement. (I now make a decent living writing about sleep health and living with multiple sclerosis.) Learn everything you can and enjoy the ride. Once you develop an expertise, many previous obstacles to the writing life melt away.

10. Have regular workouts, take regular breaks: People who lose lots of weight and keep it off go slowly and realize that going cold turkey 100% of the time isn't going to work. Borrow from what they know. A steady regimen of writing is important, but avoid burnout. Breaks refill

the creative well and improve your endurance. Schedule them as part of your mission.

11. Know thyself: Spend a little time asking yourself why you are a writer and what you want to get out of it. See how these answers relate to what you have written, are currently writing and what you'd like to be writing. Knowing this Big Picture makes it easier to complete the collage of little pictures that end up shaping a whole career.

12. Share: Once you've got some work out, share yourself. Share what you know, what you've done, your mistakes, your successes. Sharing implies you have done something worth sharing. As writers, we are doing something. Something real. Something worth sharing.

Lucky Number 13. Have faith: Creative efforts are very much like panning for gold. You'll go through a lot of silt before you find nuggets. Whether you strike a mother lode or an empty riverbed has nothing to do with your educational background. It has everything to do with persistence and belief in a positive ending. Keep digging.

I wish you all the best of luck in pursuing your writing dreams. Thanks so much for listening.

Tamara Sellman earned her BA from Columbia College in 1990, where she studied Journalism. From 2000 to 2007, she served as founder and editor of the magical realism anthology, MARGIN; it continues in archives as a worldwide resource. After retiring from MARGIN, she served as creativity coach, workshop instructor, and developmental editor for Writer's Rainbow until 2010. In 2012, she returned to college to become a sleep technologist (RPSGT, 2013) and Certified Clinical Sleep Health educator (CCSH, 2014). Also in 2013, an MS diagnosis changed her writing focus to the broader topic of chronic illness and patient empowerment. After working almost 2 years in a sleep lab, she now curates www.SleepyHeadCentral.com (since 2013), serves as web consultant to the American Sleep Apnea Association, and writes regular columns for www.MultipleSclerosis.net and www.MultipleSclerosisNewsToday.com. She works from her home in Bainbridge Island where, with her husband of 30 years, she continues her practice as writer activist in both the journalistic and creative arenas, publishing fiction, nonfiction, and poetry worldwide.

Priscilla Long

From Chaos to Creative Achievement: The 'Body of Work' Inventory

June 14, 2007

As a poet and writer I want to leave behind a meaningful body of work. So, I suspect, do most artists and aspiring artists. My own desire prompted me to launch a study of the practices of high-achieving creators (mostly painters such as Georgia O'Keeffe, though I'm a poet). These predecessor creators inspire me. Perhaps, I thought, I could ratchet up my strategies and techniques—do whatever they did—to increase my chances of leaving behind a meaningful body of work. One thing these high-level creators do is keep track of their works. They account for all their works—not just works sold or commissioned or published. Following their lead, I worked out a system for tracking the body of work I've created over the past four decades. It is remarkable how my creative inventory has helped me to deepen and extend my creative efforts. I offer the outline of my system here in case it might do the same for you.

Many high-level creators make a decision to be productive. This is a most significant decision, since they have been found to be a lot more productive than average creators. We call them high-achieving because they create more masterworks, but the interesting fact is that they also create more duds. Also, as stated above, they typically account for all their works, including duds and non-duds. High-achieving creators tend to conceive of each new work as part of a body of work created over a lifetime. Their list of works (or analogous record-keeping system) helps them to think this way. They can look at their list to see at a glance where they've been and that helps them see where next to go.

In contrast, average creators tend to forget works, abandon works, reject works, and lose works. Because of this trail of lost pieces (poems, stories, paintings, or whatever), they have a weak sense of what actually constitutes their body of work, and each new piece is brand new. Their lost poems are essentially devalued poems. (And if the poet does not value his or her own work, who will value it?) This is not to say that every poem is a good poem or a finished poem, but that any poem might be worked on (often again and again) and eventually driven into the barn of finished work. Poets who work on their craft usually gain a bit of skill each year and that skill is available for honing past work. A lost poem loses its chance at art. It is lost to the possibility of revision. The creative energy expended on it, which may have been considerable, is also lost (or at least dissipated). In contrast, Yeats (for example) continued to revise his entire body of work, including his juvenilia, throughout his lifetime.

If you work across two or more genres, as many of us do, the problem of "loss under the bed" becomes even more acute. It becomes, "Now, where was I? Uh ..."

Each artist will devise his or her own system for keeping track of works. But for any system, a few principles should be kept in mind. The first is that the creative inventory should include all the works, not just works deemed worthy. The second is that the inventory should be organized chronologically so that you can see at a glance what you were doing ten years ago or twenty years ago, and so that you will always have an ever-growing record of your productivity for the current year. Georgia O'Keeffe's system was to keep a page in a notebook for every painting she started, in which she included materials, notes, title, dimensions, where the work was located, and so on. Because she did this as she went, the notebooks, which are dated, proceed chronologically. For visual artists such a notebook will become the basis for an eventual catalogue raisonné. A visual artist will typically include a visual representation of the work as part of the inventory.

The List of Works forms the core of my own inventory system. When I first started making my list, I was astonished at how much work I was sitting on. This, it turns out, is a common astonishment for poets and writers who undertake to make a chronological list of every piece of work that has reached the point of first draft or beyond. If you've been writing for a number of years, you'll find that it will take some time to complete your list (you open another drawer only to find one more forgotten poem, one more forgotten story). However, the minute you begin to construct your list, the benefits start accruing, and once the system is set up, it's utterly simple to maintain.

The List of Works

I keep two Lists of Works, one for prose and one for poetry. These two lists literally contain every piece I've ever brought to the point of first draft or beyond. Among the items on my "List of Works—Prose" are my published history book, the draft of a novel, and a rather dreadful story I wrote in 1964, more than 40 years ago. On the "List of Works—Poetry," the earliest poem is dated summer 1970. (It's the first poem I typed out of my journal. May the untyped "poems" of the sixties rest in peace in their respective journals.) My two Lists of Work tell me that I've written 340 poems (some published, some in circulation, some in draft, some inept) and 135 prose works, including the history book and including 35 short stories (some published, some in circulation, some in draft, some inept).

What is this, quantity over quality?_Yes it is. Why does quantity matter? Well, we've seen how high-level creators create more, and we want to be high-level creators. But the speed of work is not at issue. I for one am a slow writer. And I definitely do not relish the idea of churning out slight pieces. The actual numbers matter only to the poet or writer. This is your private working tool, and the numbers it reveals are nobody's business but your own. The list allows you to see the work you've done and it signifies respect for work done. It allows you to track your yearly production. It allows you to find any given piece to take up again. The list gives you a practice that you now share with those high-achieving creators who do quantify their works. (Georgia O'Keeffe 2,045 objects; Eduardo Manet 450 oil paintings among other works; the American painter Alice Neel about 3,000 works; dare we mention Picasso? —26,000 works; the remarkable short-story writer Edith Pearlman: "Edith Pearlman has published more than 250 works of short fiction and short nonfiction." Of course that doesn't tell us how many works Pearlman has *composed*.

Essential Characteristics of the List of Works

Each title on the list and all associated information takes up one and only one line (you can clearly see the items at a glance).

The list is ordered chronologically by year, beginning with the present and working backward. Works done long ago with fuzzy dates go under decade dates (like "1980s"). As you continue to make new poems or stories it's easy to update the list, using exact dates. Every time I complete a first draft of a new work, I put it on the list, with its date of original composition (the date the first draft was completed).

The list includes the title of the piece. What to do about untitled poems? My first poetry teacher, the late Harold Bond, required us to title every poem. This is a good idea because you can use that title-space in a variety of ways, and if you make a title you don't particularly like, it's there asking to be changed to a better title. However, if you insist on untitled poems, it's conventional to use the first line, or the first part of the first line, to identify the poem.

The list includes the date of original composition. That is, when did you complete the first draft? That's the date you want. Date of "final" completion is not of interest and in any case it floats: We poets—haven't we been known to revise a poem *after* publication? As you move backward in time you will no doubt have to guess at some dates. The date you achieve that first draft is autobiographically interesting and once fixed, never has to move. (Visual artists do it a bit differently since they typically do not consider a work a work until it is finished.)

Each work has the word "published" or the word "circulating" after it, unless it is neither published nor circulating, in which case it has nothing after it. Literary writers such as poets, who are not working on commission, typically have several pieces working and some lying dormant, ready to be taken up at a later date.

Finally, the one line of information per title does not say where a piece appears if it has been published, it does not say where is circulating to, and it does not contain any sort of judgment or assessment or plan (such as "abandon?" or "revise" or "shorten?").

A piece you may never revise just sits there, like my short story written in 1964. It is part of your body of work. It shows you where you have been. For me, that first story of mine, however amateur, is a remarkable repository of threads I find woven into subsequent writing. Thus may a creator's preliminary works have interest and value. (Besides, some day I may revise that old story.)

Example of my List of Works (prose list)

2007

"My Brain on my Mind" (June-December 2007)
"From Chaos to Creative Achievement"— first comp. July 2007 PUBLISHED
"Got Manure?"—first composed June 2007
"My Old Friend" (story)—first composed March 12, 2007
"Bodies: The Exhibition"—first composed February 2007 PUBLISHED
"Purple Prose"—first composed February 2007

<u>2006</u>

Review of The Decline of Anthracite—first composed July 2006 PUB-LISHED

Stonework: Geographies of Memory (book of short nonfictions) CIR-CULATING

Piece on How I wrote "Genome Tome"—first composed May 2006 PUBLISHED

"Extending Connections, Deepening Insight" first comp May 2006 (Ch. of Begin Again)

"Frugality" (story)—first composed April/May 2006

"Worked Well With Others" Rev. of Francis Crick biog. first comp. May PUBLISHED

"The Studio"—first composed March 2006 (chapter of Creating the Creative Life)

"A Bridge to Beauty" (extreme revision of Ode)—first composed March PUBLISHED

"Studio as Brain"—first composed February 2006

<u>2005</u>

"Ode to a Bridge"—first composed (Long/O"C class) September 2005

"Anamorphosis: A Painting by Margaret Tomkins"—comp May 2005 CIRCULATING

"Space and Time"—first composed April 2005 CIRCULATING

"Living for Robert" (story)—first composed February 2005 CIRCU-LATING... etcetera

Where are these works, actually? I keep a digitalized copy, latest version only, on the computer and its printed-out hard copy in chronologically ordered three-ring binders (one for poetry, one for creative nonfictions, one for short stories). Previous drafts and marked-up workshopped copies are put far away in archive boxes or in the recycle bin. The hard copies of current versions have their date of original composition written on them.

As you begin this process of listing your works, you will make interesting discoveries, the first being the actual extent of your work to date. Another surprise for me was to find works I considered vastly inferior, requiring (I thought) massive revision, which in reality were close to complete. A lyrical essay I wrote had been gathering dust for five years. I worked on it for two hours and sent it out. It's a lovely piece (I now think) and is slated to appear in a lovely literary magazine.

Constructing your List of Works_will help you become a more aware poet, a more aware writer. Each year it will give you a measuring stick of your annual progress—defined not by the external world of prizes and publications but by you, the creator. Finally, the List of Works stands as an emblem of respect for the work. It is a creator's tool that can help artists, poets, and writers realize their dream of creating a meaningful body of work

Priscilla Long is a Seattle-based writer of poetry, creative nonfiction, science, fiction, and history. Her five books are: *Fire and Stone: Where Do We Come From? What Are We? Where Are We Going?* (University of Georgia Press), *Minding the Muse: A Handbook for Painters, Poets, and Other Creators* (Coffeetown Press), and *Crossing Over: Poems* (University of New Mexico Press). Her how-to-write guide is *The Writer's Portable Mentor: A Guide to Art, Craft, and the Writing Life.* She is also author of *Where the Sun Never Shines: A History of America's Bloody Coal Industry.* Her awards include a *National Magazine Award* and her science column, Science Frictions, ran for 92 weeks in *The American Scholar.*

Bethany Reid

One Bad Poem

June 11, 2009

If a thing is worth doing, it is worth doing badly. —G. K. Chesterton

On August 29, 2005, I decided that during the remainder of my summer break from teaching I would write one poem each day. My daughters would go back to school in a day or so (they were twelve, twelve, and six), leaving me some leisure in the month before classes began at my college. I had undertaken this practice before and called it "one bad poem" after something I once read in a self-help book, *Wishcraft*, by Bonnie Sher and Annie Gottlieb. In short, Sher and Gottlieb advise that if perfectionism keeps you from a goal, you must vow to do whatever it is you want to do—ballet, sailing, quilting, going to law school—badly. So my goal was not to write one splendid, brilliant poem per day, but simply to get up early every morning and write a draft of a very bad—terrible, if need be—poem.

My friend Glenda, who is also my massage therapist, had watched me go through this process before, and found the title "One Bad Poem" unnecessarily self-deprecating. She wanted me to call it, "One Rich Reflection on the Day." Sometimes it does turn out to be a rich reflection. Sometimes it turns out to be splendid and brilliant. But the inelegant idea of a bad poem is what gets my notebook and pen out. How can I fail? When I saw Glenda the day before classes began, that fall of 2005, she asked me how I was feeling, and I told her I was sad because the next day I would be giving up writing my one bad poem. She said, "Don't give it up! Keep writing!" Glenda is tall and willowy. She has dark eyes that crackle as often as they twinkle. I complained—I won't have time, I'm so busy, 80 to 100 students, not to mention three daughters. She would have none of it. "You have all the time there is," she said. "Write the poem. Everything else will be a snap."

It wasn't always a snap, but each day I wrote a poem and I typed it up; I put a date on it, and I put it in a notebook. I thought I'd keep up the practice for one more month, just until I saw Glenda again. Then I had a poetry reading scheduled for December third, and that became a target for when I could quit. December third came and went and I kept writing. From August 29 to the end of December I missed only two days. I wrote 123 new poems—bad poems, perhaps, but poems.

Like many writers, I have for a long, long time attempted to write every day. I write in a journal anywhere from a short entry of a few lines to three or four pages. The one-bad-poem practice did not replace journaling—what I usually call "scribbling"—and differs significantly. My journal is where I go to gripe about my kids and my husband, and sometimes to brag about them. I cry on my journal's shoulder about the washing machine not agitating right and about the freezer going out. I list things to do and things accomplished. I write about my students and my friends and the weather and what my sister said yesterday. Some of my journal entries lead to poetry, but they are not poetry. The journal is a repository, a way I have of clearing my mind so that I can get on with the day. Poems, even bad poems, feel quite different to me.

So where do the poems come from? That first fall, when Hurricane Katrina swept her way through New Orleans, I wrote a number of poems about floods, real and metaphorical. I also worked themes of heaven, marriage, housecleaning, horses, Eden, teaching, and children. I worked each theme as if it were a vein of rich ore that I was trying to chip out of myself. Some days I felt stuck. On one particular morning that first fall I gave up and checked my email. Afterwards, I wrote the first draft of this poem:

MY MOTHER EMAILS ABOUT HER NEW DISHWASHER

"The dishwasher is plumed now."
When the plumber opened its box,
the dishwasher strutted out, eyes bright
as glass beads, tail feathers of emerald

and turquoise fanning
over pale linoleum. When it leapt
shrieking to the china cabinet,

my mother and the plumber
had to coax it down—Cheerios
and Quaker Oats, a stalk of celery.

And so the dishwasher took its place,
hunkering beside the sink.
The stove stretched a striped paw

and growled. My mother paid
the plumber. She tied her apron on
and set to making supper.

Recently I've been "unwriting" poems—taking a first line or basic premise from someone else's poem and then going in the opposite direction. Here is one starting place, lines from Rainer Maria Rilke's "I Am Much Too Alone in This World, Yet Not Alone" (translated by Annamarie S. Kidder):

I want to unfold.
Nowhere I wish to stay crooked, bent;
for there I would be dishonest, untrue.
I want my conscience to be
true before you;

want to describe myself like a picture I observed
for a long time, one close up,
like a new word I learned and embraced,
like the everyday jug,
like my mother's face,
like a ship that carried me along
through the deadliest storm.

And the one-bad-poem I wrote in response:

Today I would like nothing better
than to be folded,
folded like a note slipped into a book
to mark a page you don't want to forget,
or folded like a sheet tugged from the clothesline,
in half and in half again.
I want to be folded the way egg whites
are folded into a meringue,
like sheep into a fold,
like an origami bird,
like a dollar bill into a coin purse.
Later you can take me out, unfold me,
smooth my edges and spend me
on something unexpected and delicious,
a peach or a packet of art paper
or a bar of dark chocolate
folded into its envelope of foil.

Another fertile source for new poems is, of course, my own notebooks. Failed poems make great starts for new poems. Good poems do, too. I sometimes set myself the task of using the same opening image several days in a row, or, while leafing through the typed poems, I'll stop and draft a new poem beside an old one.

Each year that I have been writing my one bad poem per day, I've been able to salvage about fifty poems, to see at least that many through to some form of completion that made it possible to put them in the mail to literary magazines and journals. The result has been, over four years, more than forty published poems, two awards, and four nominations for the (still elusive) Pushcart Prize. I don't have a new book of poems forthcoming (how I wish) but I have started a poetry blog, which you can visit at www.awriters_alchemy.blogspot.com. The writer's alchemy address was a false start—of course it's titled "One Bad Poem."

As my daughters have grown older, finding time to write has become more complex. They go to bed later and later, and I find it more and more difficult to get up early. Nevertheless, my one-bad-poem practice has kept me writing. Somehow, despite having three kids and a husband and elderly parents and friends and a teaching career, every single day I pick up my notebook and I write one bad poem. So far, so good.

MORNING POEM

I'm keeping myself as compact
as possible, a neat little house
with the doors locked
when the poem opens like a window
and in comes all this stuff I hadn't planned on—
light and birdsong and the sound
of traffic. Or the poem
isn't the window; it's everything outside
the window. The poem is a tree,
a dogwood or maple or cedar.
The poem is the breeze toying with the leaves
of the dogwood and the maple and the cedar.
The poem is the rattle
of the smaller shrubs, the salal
and Oregon grape, as the raccoons scurry through.

The poem is the motion behind
the raccoons, the mother who is large
and a little scary,
her kits who trundle after. But now
I am no longer a house. I put on
a jacket and shoes. I crawl through the window
that the poem left open as it escaped.

NOTES:

I found the Rilke lines at www.poets.org. Other on-line sources I visit frequently are poems.com (Poetry Daily) and www.duotrope.com (Duotrope Digest), both good portals to lots and lots of journal and small magazine websites.

A revised version of my poem *Folded* was accepted for Phrasings IV (2010), a dance and poetry production sponsored by Chuckanut Sandstone Poets and the Bellingham Repertory Dance Company.

Bethany Reid's most recent book of poetry is *Sparrow*, which won the 2012 Gell Poetry Prize. Her poems have appeared in numerous journals and anthologies, including *All We Can Hold, A Cadence of Hooves, Calyx, Pontoon, Cheat River Review,* and *The MacGuffin*. Although she has retired from full-time teaching, she keeps busy writing and taking care of her family, and blogs about both at http://www.bethanyareid.com.

On the Dangers of Craft

Sandi Sonnenfeld

November 14, 2002

I recently wrote a short story that failed. To write those words down on the page is clearly not an easy thing to do. No one likes to fail, especially a woman like me, who believes the work I do defines who and what I am, my place in the flotsam of life. And in contemporary America where literary success is defined by how famous you are, how big your advance, or by the number of books you have published, it's hard to admit failure at all.

The story shouldn't have failed, which is just one of the many reasons why writing is so hard. The theme, which focuses on the hypocrisy of religion in America, is significantly complex. The protagonist, a precocious nine-year-old black girl from Boston who is taken under the wing of four white born-again Christians, is smart and likable. And her four foils, each of whom I tried to develop as individuals instead of as one collective antagonist, infuse the story with both humor and simmering resentment. I worked on the story on and off again for more than eighteen months, going over each line, honing each word with precision like a dentist drilling away at decay, applied apt metaphors and employed fresh language, used repetition and rhythm in sparse appropriate ways. I relied, that is, on craft.

Part of the problem began when I realized that I had grown bored of writing the same characters with whom I had success with in the past. White women in their 20s or 30s, well-educated, middle-class, perhaps with just a trace of ethnicity, women not unlike myself, struggling with feeling isolated or cut off, working to make sense of themselves in this post-feminist world where choice abounds, yet where so many of us still remain desperately unhappy, longing for some unnamed fulfillment. I liked these women, knew them very well, worked hard to protect them, nurtured their neurosis and eccentricities, celebrated when at the end of each story, they made some small step towards self-awareness, or happiness, or freedom. These were characters that helped me publish my first two-dozen short stories, who dogged me into my recently issued memoir. But I felt it was time to let them go, to create a character completely different from myself, to write that breakout story, the one that would herald me as a fresh, new talent, a latter-day Flannery O'Connor who could write of prejudiced old ladies in purple and green hats and murderer misfits with equal enmity and compassion.

How ridiculous, you say to yourself—time or critics or readers decide whether or not you are good or new or fresh. It's not up to you, and such thoughts, therefore, are taboo, something you have no right to be messing with. Instead, you should applaud yourself for taking a risk, for trying to take yourself to the next level. You tell yourself to stop acting so foolishly, placing so much pressure on one short story, one idea.

Yes, it is. Yet for those of us who are plagued by self-doubt, who subsist on bravado rather than true courage, who still care too much about what others might think or say, such pressure bubbles and boils within us, until without warning, it rises up like a flood, casting us adrift in swift waters, drowning the more creative self, and leaving only judgment and silence in its wake.

For as I read the story over and over again, fine-tuning a particular sentence, niggling over each individual word, adding yet one more joke, clutching to craft as the oarswoman clutches for a jagged rock or stray branch as her canoe is swept down the rushing river, the focus suddenly became about my survival as a writer rather than writing itself. The story was told by someone numbed by cold and fear who had been capsized out on that river for a long time, someone who was going through the motions of creation in the hopes that creation itself would take over.

Abandoned on the cold bare riverbank, I kept trying to start a fire to warm me. But even burnished with color, a few stray leaves gathered from the riverside will never ignite if the wood beneath them is wet through.

"Now hold on, hold on," a low buzz hums in my ear. "You can't just leave it at that—comparing the craft of writing to a canoe adrift. It's facile, and just too damn obvious. You haven't yet earned it—you need to dig deeper than that—search for something richer, truer. You need a metaphor that's not been overused, comparing writing to coconuts perhaps or maybe brown mushrooms. Yes, you are a pig, a greedy pig down on the ground sniffing for truffles, your pink snout roots about in the dirt, tossing aside words like dried up weeds, searching out the few choice treats, those sweet fragile morsels that dissolve in your mouth almost before you can grasp them."

And while I am wallowing down here in the mud, my pink pig ears alert in case some other pig enters my territory, threatening to gather up truffles more effectively than me, I must admit something else as well. It's not that I wrote a single story that failed. In point of fact, since my memoir was published more than two years ago, I've yet to complete anything new. I have dozens of half-started stories, essays written three-quarters through, a novel that came to an abrupt halt in chapter three.

Even before I saw the book's four-color cover, before the reviews came in, or the book tour began, the damage was done. I was a published author, something I had dreamt of and labored over for fifteen years, and now that it had happened, I was terrified. Because now I knew just enough about craft, knew just enough about what makes narrative work, to doubt my own abilities. Now I had to deliver—whatever I wrote had to be "worthy" of a published author. Every word had to shimmer like glass, shine like fine silver, or readers would know at once that I was a fraud.

And I think that is exactly the challenge emerging writers face. Why eighty percent of all first-time novelists never publish a second book. We have learned just enough to realize how much further we need to go. We know just enough to respect and marvel at other writers' work and wonder why we ever thought we could write as well as them, or even as well as we did last year. So we cover it up, try to bury our doubt in craft. "It has to be right. It must be right. I will make it right," the litany goes in my head and with it goes spontaneity, freshness, challenge, all those reasons why I wanted to attempt such a story in the first place.

For months, I carried around the ending of the story, how I thought it must end, was slated to end, forcing the characters to go there even when they fought me, clamored for me to let them breathe. But I believed in the power of structure, in linear narrative, and was determined to put them in their place. Thus craft took me away from the organic in favor of form, in lieu of my determination that this story would be about a particular thing which I had set out to express.

Perhaps the topic of religious hypocrisy was too big for me to handle in a short story— after all, Hawthorne needed an entire novel to explore the meaning of that Scarlet A. Perhaps deep down, I really didn't know what I felt about the dangers of fundamentalism, had a visceral response, yes, but never really thought through what it meant. Certainly, I put too much emphasis on my need to write something *timely*, something *important*, a desire which in itself is deadly. All I know is that week after week as I worked on the story, moving paragraphs around, rewriting line after line, my passion for the piece, and thus the piece itself, slowly died. A sort of creeping paralysis set in. I wrote and rewrote each word, but the result was never any different, the piece never really grew legs. Yet I couldn't abandon it. This was to be my breakout story. If I couldn't do this, then, of course, I was an abject failure. I wouldn't be able to write anything else, let alone publish anything else.

When I first begin to write, I never thought about publication. Partly it was because publication was for other people, those anointed few with talent, with last names that spoke of greatness such as James, Fitzgerald, Didion and Atwood. Mostly it was because writing itself was so exciting, a chance to explore myself and other worlds at the same time that it never dawned on me that anyone but me could possibly find it of value. My head was crammed full of words, ideas, snippets of dialogue, with why one character would betray another, with how to show that betrayal. I typed away in my college dormitory on my old Smith Corona typewriter (back in the 1980s when computers were still just for math majors), the clacking keys echoing against the white-walled austerity of my room (the student next door, a pre-Med, complained to the RA how my working kept her up at night until the RA ruled that I couldn't type past midnight). Then I would lay awake in bed letting the words come at me, hungering until I could break free and give it another go first thing the next morning, eschewing my 8:35 a.m. philosophy class so that I could keep writing. I never suffered writer's block back then, never had doubts, or lacked ideas to write about, to explore. I didn't know enough about the writing process, about craft, to question doing it. I didn't know that one was supposed to build a character over time, that titles should reflect theme, or that repetition helped hold paragraphs and ideas together.

An actress friend once told me to successfully create a character we must begin as though we know nothing about the world, about narrative, about craft. Yet too often we cling to craft because we've worked so very hard to learn it in the first place. We cling to craft because it's what we have been taught in our writing workshops and panel discussions and in pompous self-help books for writers. We cling to craft because in the end, it will allow us—okay, yes, I will return to that same stale metaphor—to right that listing canoe. But in my determination to make sure that my story stayed on course, I somehow forgot why I put to sea in the first place.

Here is the lesson then, the small, glorious victory I achieved by at long last completing a new work, this essay I share with you now. The key for the writer who has started realizing publication is to trick yourself into being a beginner again, to relegate craft to the background, to revision three or four, to send it to the time-out chair, or to the locker room for a long, hot shower, so it won't corrupt that delicate, sweet moment of excitement, that first adventurous journey that must inevitably begin, "Once upon a time...."

Sandi Sonnenfeld is a fiction writer and essayist. With the publication of her memoir, *This Is How I Speak* (Seattle: Impassio Press), Sandi was named a 2002 Celebration Author by the Pacific Northwest Booksellers Association, which recognizes writers whose work merits special notice. Sandi's work has appeared in more than 30 literary magazines and anthologies, including *Sojourner, Voices West, Hayden's Ferry Review, ACM, Raven Chronicles, Necessary Fiction, Perigee, Mr. Bellers' Neighborhood* and *The Doctor TJ Eckleburg Review* among others. A graduate of Mount Holyoke College, Sandi holds an MFA in Fiction Writing from the University of Washington, where she won the Loren D. Milliman Writing Fellowship. She's currently working on an historical novel set in 17th century Russia. For more, visit authorsandisonnenfeld.com.

About the editors

Working on the Anthology at Esther's house: Katie Tynan, Peggy Sturdivant, Esther Altshul Helfgott (March 2017)

Esther Altshul Helfgott is a nonfiction writer & poet with a Ph.D. in history from the University of Washington. She is the author of *Listening to Mozart: Poems of Alzheimer's* (Yakima, WA: Cave Moon Press, 2014); *Dear Alzheimer's: A Caregiver's Diary & Poems* (Yakima, WA: Cave Moon Press, 2013); *The Homeless One: A Poem in Many Voices* (Seattle: Kota Press, 2000) and the blog, "Witnessing Alzheimer's: A Caregiver's View" (Seattle Post-Intelligencer, 2008 – 2015). In 2010, she was a Jack Straw poet. Her work appears in *American Imago: Psychoanalysis and the Human Sciences*; *Beyond Forgetting: Poetry and Prose about Alzheimer's Disease*; *BlackPast: Remembered & Reclaimed*; *Blue Lyre Review*; *Cirque: A Literary Journal for the North Pacific Rim*; *Floating Bridge Review*; *HistoryLink.org*; *Journal of Poetry Therapy*; *Pontoon*; *Raven Chronicles*, *Ribbons*

& others. She is a 2010 Jack Straw poet and founder of the *It's About Time Writers" Reading Series,* now in its twenty-ninth year. She loves the Poetry Pole her children built her for Mother's Day.

Peggy Sturdivant: is founder of the Ballard Writers Collective, and she is a longstanding columnist for *The Ballard News-Tribune.* In 2012, six years after the Ballard Branch of Seattle Public Library gave the series a home, along with Katie Tynan, Sturdivant took over curating the It's *About Time Writers' Reading Series.* She had connected with Seattle's writing community through the late Pesha Gertler's "Self-Discovery for Women through Creative Writing" class in 1997, although her need to write dated back to elementary school. Sturdivant was a 2002 Jack Straw Writer and is co-author of the non-fiction book *Out of Nowhere* (Lazy Jane, 2010). She hopes her writing will survive the demise of the local newspaper. As a teacher, Sturdivant works with writers ages five to ninety-five. She facilitates "Writing for the Moment" classes at Cancer Lifeline and works with Sara Yamasaki's Moving Words Writing Clinics

Katie Tynan: "I knew of *It's About Time* by reputation and longevity when Peggy approached me in 2011 to help with the transition of the long-running series. I started attending right away and what riches of information about writing and support for my own writing I found! I'd been working as a freelance writer but that was a lonely business being just me and my computer day after day. *At It's About Time,* I found a diverse community of people interested both in writing themselves and in hearing what others were writing. In embracing the challenge of getting up in front of a crowd as emcee, I found myself able to get up at Open Mic. My growth as a poet has improved tremendously for this experience. Although other projects pulled me away from being co-curator after 3 great years, the second Thursday of the month is always written in pen in my calendar. I can't say enough about both Esther and Peggy for their efforts in bringing this gem to our community."

Acknowledgements

We are appreciative of all the venues that provided our roving reading series with homes: Ravenna-Eckstein Community Center; North Seattle Community College's Rose Room; Globe Bookstore and café on 'the Ave'; Seattle Public Library's University, Greenwood and Northeast branch, and Diane Nordfors' Other Voices Book Store on NE 65th Street; Ravenna Third Place Books; Open Books: a poem emporium which allowed us to have a benefit to raise money to publish the It's About Time newsletters (deposited in the Archives at Suzzallo library, University of Washington). Special thanks to Chris Higachi and Lynn Miller for work to provide It's About Time with a permanent home at the Ballard branch of the Seattle Public Library. And to Crysta Casey (1952 - 2008) who helped keep the series going from the first time she read at the University branch library in the early nineties. Thank you to all the readers and the audiences who continue to listen, to share at the open mic and create the most supportive and welcoming writers' reading series in Seattle. To you we give a collective hug.

Esther, Peggy and Katie

Made in the USA
Lexington, KY
30 October 2019